D0055832

WITHDRAWN

Modern Drama and the Death of God

George E. Wellwarth

THE UNIVERSITY
OF WISCONSIN
PRESS

MODERN DRAMA

and the

DEATH OF GOD

Published 1986

The University of Wisconsin Press
114 North Murray Street
Madison, Wisconsin 53715

The University of Wisconsin Press, Ltd.
1 Gower Street
London WC1E 6HA, England

First printing

Printed in the United States of America

For LC CIP information see the colophon

ISBN 0-299-10850-3

For
Martha Sobotka Wellwarth Pressler
and for
Joseph Pressler

Contents

Preface

A word of caution is in order for the reader of this book. It is *not* intended to be a survey, critical or otherwise, of the modern drama. Hence the reader should not be either surprised or disappointed to find some of his favorite works by the authors treated in the book unmentioned or obviously important figures of the modern drama such as Chekhov, Gorki, Cocteau, or Giraudoux omitted. I have chosen to write about certain figures and certain plays that most clearly illustrate the thesis of this book. This is not to say that that thesis could not be traced in the works of other writers or in the texts of other plays: merely that the plays and authors I have chosen to write about reflect that thesis most clearly. One of my purposes in writing this book, indeed, has been to encourage the application of its theories to other authors and other plays: to encourage a reexamination of the modern drama. My principal purpose has been the identification and explication of what I believe to be the turning point in the history of ideas and, therefore, in the human attitude to reality. The resulting trend is not, of course, reflected only in the drama, and it is for this reason that I have also adduced the evidence of the novel in a couple of instances. Dramatic literature and, indeed, any art form is only one of the many ways in which intellectual trends may be observed in the development of social phenomena. It is my hope that this book will do its bit in turning literary criticism away from the isolationism imposed on it by postmodernistic and deconstructionist cliques. The necessity for clear writing increases in direct proportion to the difficulty of the subject matter to be explicated. Better to remain silent than deliberately to obscure the intellectual atmosphere with verbal smoke signals. The history of the development of human ideas is a subject that can be approached from many directions—literature, dramatic or otherwise, is only one of them. It is a subject that can be written about with crystalline clarity. And it is the only subject the careful and critical study of which has a chance of leading us into the avoidance of error in the future.

It remains for me to note only that the word "Man" is used in this work in the generic sense for linguistic convenience.

I would like to thank the many people who read this work and gave me their opinions of it in its various stages, chief among whom are my wife, Pamela, to whom more than I can set down here is owed, my colleague Professor Haskell Block, Professor Edward Margolies of the College of Staten Island, Professor Leo Hamalian of the City University of New York and Professor Thor Gabrielsen of the Sagene College of Education in Oslo. My former students Dr. Robin Hirsch and Dr. Ian Steadman also read this work in early versions and were good enough to suggest I rewrite it.

Modern Drama and the Death of God

Introduction

Philosophically speaking, modern drama is an extended meditation on existential rootlessness. It is a critical analysis of Man in the Void. The void is the comfortless realm of existential solitude into which man was cast by the death of religion. In that solitude man had to face himself, to realize that he is a microcosmic universe that takes precedence for him over all the other discrete microcosmic universes as well as over the unknowable yet enveloping macrocosmic one, that the individual is not only more important than the universal but is for all practical purposes unrelated to it. It followed, further, that he had to work out his own persona and his own fate, to weigh each contemplated action on its merits as defined by himself, to

4 Modern Drama and the Death of God

take full responsibility for it, and to be answerable to the only arbiter he could know: himself. In short, the loss of faith in religion created what was to become known as Existential Man.

Existential Man may best be defined as man without benefit of the consolations of religion. He is secular man—man with the transcendental dimension removed from his imaginative life and the sacramental dimension from his temporal life. The birth of secular man was a philosophical one; and philosophical births tend to be long and painful. At least, so it seems. The truth is that the births are usually sudden and unnoticed, the more so as the birth announcements tend to be suppressed.

Philosophies, however, are not the ultimate causes of human behavior: they are no more than interpretations of reality, attempts at abstract systematizations of altered perceptions of man's place in the universe. Philosophical viewpoints, in other words, are social artifacts. Overt changes in social reality are caused by specific political events, which, in turn, are made possible by what we may call the underlying subconscious (i.e., as yet not consciously realized) mind-set of society. This social mind-set is in turn caused by the filtering down to the collective popular mind of the consequences of scientific discovery.

The replacement of the geocentric theory of the universe with the heliocentric was the turning point of human history. The mental attitude of the human being to the cosmos, to the world, to society, to his fellow beings, to himself was necessarily qualitatively different before and after that event. If an exact moment for the beginning of modern times must be chosen, then it was surely the moment that Nicholas Copernicus finally admitted to himself, with what must have been a nicely balanced mixture of intellectual exhilaration and painful moral struggle, that the earth does indeed revolve around the sun and that man is therefore not the center of the universe. It is true that before Copernicus not only the heliocentric theory but the possibility of an infinite universe and a plurality of planetary worlds had been broached and toyed with as an intellectually amusing paradox or stimulating hypothesis. It was Nicholas of Cusa (1401–1464), a German bishop, who apparently originated the famous statement that "The universe is an infinite sphere having its centre everywhere and its circumference nowhere."[1] The difference in the case of Copernicus was not that he was a scientist in the modern sense and arrived at his conclusion by way of empiric proof rather than through abstract contemplation or intuition. The reverse was true, as a matter of fact: Copernicus retained important aspects of the Ptolemaic system and unquestioningly accepted basic Aristotelian tenets, notably that the circle was the perfect form and therefore the shape of the planetary paths around the sun. During his whole career he recorded only twenty-seven direct astronomical observations of his own. The entire Copernican system, in fact, "was based on the observational data of Ptolemy, Hipparchus and other Greek and Arab astronomers, whose statements he had uncritically accepted as Gospel truth."[2] The difference in the case of Copernicus was that he was serious about his speculations. Despite the preface to his great work, the *De Revolutionibus Orbium Coelestium*, written, possibly without Copernicus' approval or even knowledge, by Andreas Osiander, a Protestant divine, in which it was asserted that the heliocentric theory was to be considered purely as a hypothesis, Copernicus clearly thought that the motion of the earth around the sun was an incontrovertible physical fact and not a hypothesis, "a mere mathematical convenience."[3] Copernicus "repeatedly affirmed that the earth *really* moved, and thereby exposed his whole system to judgement based on real, physical considerations."[4] That conviction of Copernicus's, however "unscientifically" we may consider him to have arrived at it, together with Brahe's meticulous astronomical observations and Kepler's calculations of the planetary orbits, Galileo's confirmations and additions, Newton's cosmological demonstrations, and Laplace's elimination of Newton's pious caveats, toppled the mind-set in which religion had been comfortably ensconced for so long.[5]

It is almost impossible for us who have been immersed since birth, however uneasily and uncomprehendingly, in a spatial and temporal infinity to imagine the state of mind of those who lived before and who believed space to be finite and spherical and time to have a beginning and an end. The heliocentric theory ripped man from the security of a spatial and temporal womb to project him into a universe whose infinity condemned him to eternal helpless infancy. There can be no question that "the whole of ancient and medieval . . . theology would have taken a very different shape, if an infinite Space without centre or circumference, had been all along accepted as an obvious and unquestionable datum."[6]

Although as early as the thirteenth century some theologians had brought up the possibility of an infinite universe and had postulated a plurality of worlds as a theoretical possibility "by adducing the infinite power of God,"[7] it was not until Galileo spelled out the concrete implications that the Copernican theory had given these pious speculations that the church woke up to the potential of temporal inconvenience inherent in the concept of divine omnipotence as seen from this point of view. In a pamphlet he wrote on the interpretation of the Bible, Galileo asserted that "while the Bible could not err its exponents might, and that no effect of nature of which the senses afforded evidence, or which was a necessary conclusion from that evidence, should be considered doubtful because the Scriptures seemed to state the contrary."[8] This implied that the Bible's truth was undiscoverable because it could be transmitted only through its interpreters, who were—or, at best, might be—fallible. Furthermore, Galileo maintained that the Copernican system was confirmed by empiric evidence, which would inevitably refute the statement made in the Book of Joshua that the sun and moon were stopped in their courses at Joshua's command, if that statement were taken literally. In other words, Galileo had proclaimed the superiority of individual intelligence backed by empiric observation over the voice of traditional authority. Books were not widely read in the sixteenth and seventeenth centuries, Copernicus' hardly at all, not even by Galileo.[9] How, then, did the knowledge of the Copernican theory spread, and why were the church authorities so alarmed by Galileo's pamphlet on biblical interpretation? The answer to the second question is that Galileo did not present his views as a hypothesis, as Copernicus apparently had done, thanks to Osiander's cautious preface. The answer to the first one was best put by Arthur Koestler:

> How was it possible that the faulty, self-contradictory Copernican theory, contained in an unreadable and unread book, rejected in its time, was to give rise, a century later, to a new philosophy which transformed the world? The answer is that the details did not matter, and that it was not necessary to read the book to grasp its essence. Ideas which have the power to alter the habits of human thought do not act on the conscious mind alone; they seep through to those deeper strata which are indifferent to logical contradictions. They influence not some specific concept, but the total outlook of the mind.[10]

The theories that Galileo propounded in his pamphlet destroyed the wonderfully protean validity of that enigmatic repository of hermeneutic infinity, the Holy Bible, the authority of which had always depended on a jealously preserved hermetic "meaning" continually wrenched and twisted to the exigencies of temporal necessity. With the contradiction of one of its few unequivocal passages, the possibilities inherent in that plasticity of interpretation, formerly practiced with such ironclad impunity from secular critical scrutiny, were measurably dimmed. What the leaders of the church were afraid of was the unknown territory into which the unrestrained use of reason, unshackled by theological a priori assumptions, might lead men. Heliocentrism and infinity implied the possibility of infinite worlds served by an infinite number of clergies; and the consequent possibility that this world's clergy had only an infinitely small share of the divine attention. Clearly, this was intolerable; and those, like Giordano Bruno, who broached the subject could not be tolerated. Giordano Bruno was without doubt one of the most original thinkers of the sixteenth century, which closed with his death at the stake in 1600. He was by no means the first to broach the possibility of an infinite universe, but he was the first to preach it far and wide as a doctrine and to popularize it for the thinking public in literary form with a powerfully argued theological underpinning.

Bruno made it possible to contemplate living in a cosmic context that was previously unimaginable, a context where there was ". . . no centre and no circumference; but the centre is everywhere, and every part is outside some other part."[11]

Scientific discoveries provide the impetus for thought, but it is the literary and philosophical thinkers who disseminate them—who, in other words, make mankind aware of the consequences implicit in the discoveries. Bruno worked out the implications of Copernicus' discovery and was able to affirm his formulations even to the point of martyrdom. Not all thinkers were able to contemplate living in an infinity without center or circumference with such cold-blooded equanimity. Less than a century after Bruno went to the stake for his assertions, Blaise Pascal was frantically trying to shore up the crumbling walls of traditional thought in his *Pensées*, written, to borrow a phrase from the future, in fear and trembling. For our purposes there are two extremely significant aspects to Pascal's methodology: his insistence on reason as the most effective path to an apprehension of God and his unquestioning acceptance of cosmic infinity. Bruno's seed had taken root. Equally significant is Pascal's motive: the urgency with which he felt constrained to prove the existence of God. To feel the necessity of logically proving the reality of that which had previously been accepted as a given aspect of the natural order, of proving that there was indeed a natural order, of analyzing and explaining the ineffable, was a sign of the extent to which the worm of doubt had burrowed into and undermined the seemingly solid and eternal bastion of unquestioning faith.

Pascal is known to most people as the originator of Pascal's Wager. This curious and both morally and intellectually pusillanimous formulation suggests that one should bet on God's existence by always acting as if his existence were in fact known. In this way one had an absolutely hedged bet: if God does not exist, one's death is a transition to oblivion, exactly like the nonbeliever's; but if he does exist, one's death is a transition to eternal bliss (the jackpot) while the nonbeliever taps out and is cast into hell. To believe in God, in other words, is to hold a potential royal flush while ignoring the possibility that there may be no game going on at all. To read Pascal nowadays, however, is to become conscious of the fact that his Wager is less significant than what we might call Pascal's Paradox, which is, simply, that he was a man obsessed with quintessentially modern problems attempting to solve them with the forms of medieval thought. The words Pascal chose to describe human existence, "nothingness, forlornness, inadequacy, impotence, and emptiness," would be attributed to Samuel Beckett by any knowledgeable modern reader, as would his remark that "The natural misfortune of our mortal and feeble condition is so wretched that when we consider it closely nothing can console us."[12] Again, we seem to hear a purely modern existential despair in the lament "When I consider the short duration of my life, swallowed up in the eternity before and after, . . . engulfed in the infinite immensity of space of which I am ignorant and which knows me not, I am frightened . . ."[13] No wonder that Pascal concluded, as so many have after him: "Man's condition: instability, *ennui*, unrest"[14] and "The eternal silence of these infinite spaces fills me with fear."[15] Pascal's words remain contemporary. He stated the problem, defined the root of the intellectual malaise of modern times; and his attempt to solve the problem foundered on its overwhelming incomprehensibility. When the philosophes came along in the next century the problem was neatly sidestepped with the almost comically evasive "solution" of the Watchmaker God, a device that shoved the transcendental question off into a remote corner while thinkers concerned themselves with the temporal problems. The philosophes prepared the intellectual groundwork for the cataclysm of the French Revolution, which demonstrated to the populace as a whole that the concept of God was an accidental and not an essential. It was not until Kafka that literature would again be faced with Pascal's problem: ". . . the predicament of a man who, endowed with an insatiable appetite for transcendental certainty, finds himself in a world robbed of all spiritual possessions."[16]

Copernicus had planted the seed, his followers in the scientific community had tended it, Bruno and Pascal had explained the effects of the planting to the layman; and with the

French Revolution it burst into full flower. The men who brought about the French Revolution had little or no consciousness of the scientific discoveries that had paved the way for their actions. But their actions could have been possible only within the parameters of the social context in which they found themselves. And that social context was the direct result of the scientific discoveries that had slowly and insidiously loosed the collective human psyche from the moorings of religion and cast it adrift on the boundless ocean of doubt.

Historically, the French Revolution was a unique event that had effects which were not to be duplicated until the First World War. What the French Revolution accomplished was the elimination of the doctrine of the divine right of kings as a meaningful concept in social thought. More precisely, it was a sudden and utterly traumatic departure from a concept that had always, ever since the first consolidation of society in neolithic times, formed the basis of law and of the cement that held disparate groups of people together in a more or less willing cohesive social whole. The unity of the sacred and the temporal had been based on an ultimately spurious concept, to be sure: a collusion between a priesthood whose power had originally been based on mastery of a primitive form of astronomy and consequent predictive powers about agricultural cycles, and hunting leaders who, their weaponry having become largely useless in an agricultural society, placed those weapons in a new perspective by creating armies and police forces. Society came to be created out of a combination of stargazing and ennui.

The French Revolution did not, of course, spell the end of society. It spelled the end of the traditional basis of society. The cohesiveness of social forms continued to be as necessary as ever, but now it could no longer be based on an unquestioning acceptance of what had been thought to be an immutable and divinely sanctioned law. It had to be based on what might be called the doctrine of convenience. One aspect of this doctrine, of course, was the continuance of the fiction (as it had now become) of divine order. The death of God, that doctrine momentarily fashionable among new-wave, laid-back theologians acquainted with the work of Friedrich Nietzsche at third hand, began in 1543 with the publication of Copernicus' discoveries. After what Milton in another context described as "a long day's dying," it culminated in the raucous death rattle of the French Revolution, whose theorists were either explicitly atheists or unconsciously satirized traditional belief in God with their creation of a substitute and essentially secular *Être Suprême* or Goddess of Reason. Nevertheless, precisely as Nietzsche foresaw, his animated mummy continues to be trotted out for acceptance as the real thing by interested parties such as popes, backwoods snake handlers, and evangelistic panhandlers, whose survival depends on the perpetuated clanking of the antiquated celestial machinery.[17] Churches, Nietzsche remarked, are the tombs and sepulchers of God.[18] What Nietzsche meant, of course, was not that God had turned out to be mortal, but that he had never been there in the first place, his presumed existence having always necessarily relied on mystical explanations; and mystical explanations, having no concrete referent, are always intrinsically meaningless: mere verbal structures with no more solidity than smoke. "God is dead" means, simply, that the concept of God is no longer credible.[19]

Another aspect of the doctrine of convenience is the recognition of the fact that human beings in general crave enslavement—that is, freedom from the responsibility of deciding the nature of their own actions. A surrogate is necessary; and thus governments, whether they be dictatorships or not, persist. For the masses it does not make much difference if the government claims authority "by the grace of God" or by the mandate of the people themselves. The point is that the necessity of existential decisions is avoided.

Artistically speaking, the period since the French Revolution has been characterized by romanticism, partially a desperate nostalgia for an imagined absolute and partially a deification of sublimated sexual relations; and by existentialism, the search for individual compromises with reality or, in Kierkegaard's perversion, the self-contradictory opting for individual religious faith. Romanticism produced no dramatic art worth the name, and as a philosophical trend proved to be no more than a temporary stopgap. It was essentially the leisure class's spurious rebellion against the drabness of life brought about by the Industrial Revolution.

Existentialism, unlike romanticism, was a genuine response to reality. Its genuineness consisted in its recognition of the fact that an irreversible change had occurred in the nature of reality, that reality as it had traditionally been looked on, in other words, simply did not exist, never had existed, and was a delusive phantom conjured up by an unholy alliance of power and necromancy. For the responsible thinker, therefore, it became necessary, as a matter of intellectual honesty and self-responsibility, to seek a reality more in accordance with the observed facts that the destruction of the old order—the *ancien régime*—had unveiled. Easier said than done. Observed facts are open to interpretation and are all too often metamorphosed by the intellectual predilections of the viewer. This happened in the case of Kierkegaard, for example. More honest was the perception that without the spurious cohesiveness that had been given them by the artificial cement of religion, the observed facts did not seem to make any sense at all. Reality was as merciful as Russian roulette and as rational as the Monte Carlo variety. This perception gave birth to two principal philosophical attitudes that have dominated dramatic literature to the present day: fragmentation and analysis.[20] In order to understand fragmentational and analytic thinking we must keep in mind that "The central fact of modern history in the West . . . is unquestionably the decline of religion."[21] I have already explained how this came about through the scientific and French revolutions; but a purely historical account can give no idea of how profound what we might call the "culture shock" was, how radical the psychological adjustment. In earlier times religion had been "a solid psychological matrix surrounding the individual's life from birth to death, sanctifying and enclosing all its ordinary and extraordinary occasions in sacrament and ritual."[22] It was as if each individual were in possession of a wonderful, magical map that gave the exact configuration of the known universe, of heaven, hell, and all the regions in between. On this map each person could instantly find his own position in space and time and could also see where he had been and what options he had for the future. A universal map, in other words, that showed *everything* and authoritatively answered that most basic of all questions, What does it all mean? And if anyone found his map too complicated to read, he could always go to his ever-available, ever-helpful, friendly local professional map reader, known to him and his fellows as the parish priest, and have it fully explained to him. There was no mystery. Everything was as clear as crystal; as clear, indeed, as the crystal sphere that bounded and enclosed the cosmos, making of it a shiny and fondly favored ornament in God's playroom. After the French Revolution had demonstrated that God was not *necessary* (though still fervently desired), all this changed. The infinitely detailed and ever-reliable map was simply no longer there. All that remained was a blank space. Faced with this, one could adopt an optimistic attitude, as the analytic thinkers did, and see an opportunity to draw a new map that depicted reality as it was. Decisions about life and reality were now in the hands of the individual, who would solve the problems of existence as seemed best to him. The other possibility was to adopt a pessimistic attitude, to despair. The fragmentational thinker either tore up the blank map in rage and disillusionment or refused to face it or sardonically drew a deliberately falsified picture of a reality that he found ultimately incomprehensible.[23]

CHAPTER 1

Fragmentation

August Strindberg is the "father" of the drama of the self. It has frequently been pointed out by critics that Strindberg was clearly paranoid to the point of being, at least at certain very obviously defined periods of his life, clinically insane. These same critics have been unanimous in pointing out that this fact is not relevant to Strindberg's stature as an artist. In fact, it has become virtually a critical credo that a writer's insanity may be mentioned for explicatory purposes only but may not be used in making value judgments of the work. This seems to me a highly debatable dogma that is badly in need of challenge, and I shall return to it shortly.

It is arguable that Strindberg never wrote about anything at all except himself, and that objective reality existed for him only insofar as it affected him. This is not the same as perceiving reality exclusively through one's own eyes. Everyone does that. It is transmuting reality from object into subject and making it the morally responsible agent for one's actions. In withdrawing within himself and making his own psyche the microcosm of the universe and the whole range of his field of inquiry and interest, Strindberg involuntarily encapsulated the malaise of the times: with the traditional points of reference removed from the outside world, with no map to consult as to the ultimate configuration of reality and one's place in it, the thinker could either distort the reality he saw, symbolically destroy it, or ignore it. Strindberg chose to ignore it. Reading Strindberg's plays and such personal, nondramatic statements as *Inferno,* one senses that he really believed that only *he* existed. With traditional philosophy in a state of flux amounting to chaos, the inner self had come to seem the only area still worthy of potentially fruitful exploration.

Strindberg's emphasis on inner exploration can be seen in all three types of drama that he wrote. In his best-known plays, the psychological domestic dramas such as *Miss Julie, The Father, Dance of Death, Creditors,* and *Comrades,* Strindberg is not, as has too often been supposed, giving us profoundly observed psychological analyses of human relations. Indeed, a separate study could profitably be made of public relations in artistic criticism. In Strindberg's case, at least, he probably attained sacred-cow status partially as the result of the notoriety he obtained through his self-pitying antics, alternating between lamentations in the style of Job and chest-puffing defiance in the style of Jove, which in retrospect made him look like a precursor of Camus' Sisyphus and *l'homme révolté* combined; and partially as a result of his undoubted foreshadowing of the German expressionist movement. What Strindberg really gives us in these psychological domestic dramas are externalizations of his own attitudes to domestic and sexual relations. *Miss Julie* and *The Father* show a savage hatred and contempt of woman unmatched since the diatribes of some of the more energetically neurotic early church fathers. There is

nothing in these plays with which a normally constituted person (specifically, in this case, a person not helplessly gripped by
misogyny) can empathize. Admirers of *Miss Julie, The Father,*
and *Dance of Death* have mistaken intensity for incisiveness and
baffled rage for psychological insight. The Swedish critic Victor Svanberg is the only writer known to me to have perceived
the truth about Strindberg's "insight":

> Strindberg is the personification of everything that is bar-
> baric in the Swedish character. . . . We proudly parade him
> before the world as the quintessence of Swedish culture. It is
> hard to think of a better way to parade Swedish unculture.
> . . . [A] simpler way of accounting for the applause with
> which women greeted *Miss Julie* and *Dance of Death* is to
> assume every woman is a masochist at heart—a statement
> which I, for one, believe applies only to a vanishing breed of
> women. I venture to offer a . . . rather more complicated
> explanation. Women approve of the marital squabbles in
> Strindberg because the squabbles enable them to triumph
> over this alleged titan in his lifelong, desperate and forever
> futile attempts to settle his accounts with the weaker sex. We
> have to look long and hard for better proof of woman's
> triumph over man than Strindberg's misogyny.[1]

This seems to me an extremely acute analysis; nor does its
obviously polemic intent detract from its critical acuteness.
Feminine attitudes have changed considerably since Svanberg
wrote this in 1931, and what was a psychologically perceptive
observation then is perhaps no longer valid now. Women no
longer need to gloat over Strindberg's misogyny in order to
achieve a vicarious feeling of triumph over men. Strindberg's
railings against women and his distorted portrayal of them as
domesticated harpies are simply no longer of interest to
women. Women can now afford to ignore Strindberg, or, at
most, to smile at his impotent rancorousness as a caricature of
the "stronger" sex. For men Strindberg's characters have become no less psychologically invalid than for women. The
female characters are in any case totally unreal puppetlike
emanations of the Strindbergian man's viewpoint. Only the
male characters in Strindberg are fully realized psychological

portraits—and they are all, without exception, concrete manifestations of one or another of the author's misogynistic obsessions. While they are fully realized psychological portraits,
they are portraits of madmen. Strindberg, however, does not
intend them to be seen as madmen: he intends them to be seen
as eminently sane but driven mad by diabolic feminine plots.
The Father and *Dance of Death* are almost comically piteous pleas
for empathy with these incredible figures, who are no more
than autobiographical self-justifications. On the other side of
the coin we have a figure like the manservant in *Miss Julie*, who
is no more than a wish-fulfillment figure in the form of an
irresistible phallic robot. In this connection it is significant that
Strindberg titled one of his autobiographical works *Son of a
Servant* and that his first wife was, like Miss Julie, a member of
the minor nobility. One soon tires of observing clinical psychological studies whose traits are exaggerated to the point of
absurdity.

On the other hand, while the psychological validity of
Strindberg's domestic plays is effectively nonexistent, they
have considerable thematic importance as way stations on the
crumbling road of artistic fragmentation. They mirror, in the
realm of imagination, the collapse caused by the disappearance of one after another of the a priori foundation stones on
which the philosophical edifice—that miraculously levitated
pyramid of inverted principles covered with rococo curlicues
of fanciful thought—had rested for so long. Strindberg's
domestic plays have held the stage because of the single-
minded emotional intensity with which they are imbued and
because of the dazzling effect such intensity in the hands of
virtuoso actors has on the minds of audiences. The less said
about less than virtuoso performances of Strindberg the better. The significance of plays like *The Father, Dance of Death,* and
most particularly *Miss Julie* lies in their implicit assumption that
the two institutions on which society as we have always known it
is principally based—the family and the distinctions of social
rank—are a carefully contrived fiction. In *The Father* and *Dance
of Death* marriage and family life are treated as farcical in the
ideal sense and a baseless pretense in the practical sense. It

would be a serious mistake to underestimate the radicalness of Strindberg's thought here. Whatever his faults as a psychologist and as a playwright may have been, he was an instinctive prophet who propounded his ideas with the relentless single-mindedness of genius. What Strindberg did in those two plays and what he did in a comic vein in *Comrades* had simply not been done before. He proclaimed the nullity of the institution of marriage and showed the possibilities of a social situation that had had all its traditional props pulled out from under it. Depressing though Strindberg's vision may have been and motivated though it may have been by his personal discontents, he paved the way for the excoriations of the expressionists and the elimination of the theme of married love and familial relationships from the bulk of the twentieth-century intellectual drama. It should be noted that Nora's slamming of the door on her ninny of a husband in Ibsen's play has nothing at all to do with the socially iconoclastic attitude that Strindberg pioneered. Ibsen was writing a play that pointed up the deficiencies of the contemporary marriage relationship and implied the remedy. He was trying to patch up a structure the existence of which Strindberg explicitly denied.

Miss Julie was quite as radical a play as *The Father* and *Dance of Death;* and, unlike the other two, a viable stage play that represented perhaps the only occasion on which Strindberg was able to rise above his obsessions and give us psychologically credible characterizations. Its importance lies in its stark and uncompromising depiction of the sex drive as superior to and destructive of class distinctions. The class distinctions on which society had always heretofore been based simply do not exist except insofar as they are so deeply ingrained that they triumph over natural instincts. We see this in Jean's absurd cringing, which he recognizes as unnatural, at the mere mention of the Count's presence. But the daughter's sexual union with him effectively points up, as Schnitzler was to do some years later in a more cynical way with *Reigen,* the essential nonexistence of any rational basis for the cringing. As Jean puts it in the key line of the play, "I have no . . . ancestry . . . but I can become an ancestor myself." And just as the "nobility" of

Julie's ancestry is spurious, so is the attitude to life that is based on a recognition of that "nobility" and the distinctions that go with it. *Miss Julie* created its own descendants, as did *The Father* and *Dance of Death,* in the drama that was to come.

The second type of drama Strindberg wrote was the drama of conscious self-analysis as opposed to the unconscious self-analysis we have in the domestic dramas. The best-known plays in this group are the three plays entitled *To Damascus.* In these plays the protagonist, known as the Stranger, is frankly a self-portrait of Strindberg. As the title indicates, these are plays about a pilgrimage toward salvation. During his pilgrimage the Stranger is constantly encountering the Lady, an obvious composite portrait of Strindberg's first and second wives, Siri von Essen and Frieda Uhl, with the latter predominating; many of the incidents are directly drawn from Strindberg's real-life relationship with his second wife. The title further indicates Strindberg's megalomaniac comparison of himself and his imagined salvation (Part 3 ends with the Stranger's mock funeral and presumed rebirth after his definitive rejection of the Tempter, an alter ego) with Saul of Tarsus' conversion and sanctification. A good case could be made out for St. Paul's having been a paranoid schizophrenic, but that is not, of course, how Strindberg saw him. Important for the effect of these plays on subsequent drama is the fact that everything that happens is seen from the Stranger's viewpoint and interpreted with reference to him. The function of all of the other characters, when they are not like the Tempter actually portraits of other aspects of The Stranger's state of mind, is to minister to the protagonist and illuminate aspects of his self. The religious conversion at the end of Part 3 is spurious: it is actually an affirmation of faith in himself by the protagonist. The setting of the play has become the protagonist's own mind: everything that happens does so because he has willed it and is treated solely as it affects him: object has become subject. The spurious affirmation of faith at the end is actually a rejection of faith in the conventional sense. All three parts build up toward this statement of the uselessness, hostility, and incomprehensibility of the outside world, and of the necessity for faith in oneself, in the inviolability and existential validity of the inner self. Human experience in Strindberg becomes something that is confined to the writhings of the cerebral cortex.

In *To Damascus*, Part 1, there is a passage that neatly combines this reference of everything outside to the inner self with Strindberg's characteristic fearful and contemptuous attitude toward women:

> STRANGER: What is it you are crocheting? Like one of the three Fates of old, you sit passing the yarn between your fingers. . . . But don't stop . . . The most beautiful thing I know is a woman busy with her work or her child. What is it you are crocheting?
>
> LADY: It is . . . it is nothing but a piece of needlework . . .
>
> STRANGER: It looks like a network of knots and nerves, in which your thoughts are being woven. I imagine that is how the inside of your brain looks . . .
>
> LADY: I only wish I possessed half as much as you seem to think I have! But my mental power is nil.[2]

A few lines later the Stranger receives a letter which he believes contains money from royalties for his writing—again an obvious autobiographical reference. The letter turns out to contain merely a royalty statement to the effect that sales have been bad and no money is due. Strindberg converts this purely personal disaster into an insult from heaven and strikes a grandiose pose of defiance, as if the sole concern of heaven were Strindberg's royalties:

> STRANGER: . . . This was forever my Achilles heel! I have steadfastly borne everything—except this fatal lack of money—which always strikes me when most in need.
>
> LADY: Forgive me for asking, but how much did you receive?
>
> STRANGER: . . . What is this? No money—only a royalty statement—informing me that no money is due me. . . . Can this be right? . . . I am a doomed soul . . . But I catch the curse with two fingers and fling it back on the magnanimous giver . . . followed by my curse!
>
> LADY: Don't, don't! I am afraid of you!

STRANGER: . . . The gauntlet has been thrown and now you shall see grappling between giants! (*Unbuttoning his coat and waistcoat, with a challenging glance at the sky.*) Now—come! Strike me with your lightning and your thunder, if you dare! Frighten me with your storm, if you have the power![3]

There is a similar passage in *Inferno:* Strindberg seems to have been obsessed with the idea that thunderstorms were aimed personally at him:

> That night between midnight and two o'clock, there was a terrible storm. Such storms usually exhaust themselves quickly and pass on. This one hung over my village for two hours. I took it as a personal attack. None of the lightning flashes aimed at me succeeded in reaching their target.[4]

Again we have here the feeling so typical of Strindberg that even the most tremendous, the most obviously objectively real external phenomena occur solely with reference to him, are manufactured, so to speak, to act as mirrors of his internal wrestlings.

In Strindberg this retreat into the self has clearly evident psychological reasons; in the writers influenced by him, the German expressionists, it is deliberately done for sociophilosophical reasons.[5] Strindberg wrote about nothing but himself, and while much of his writing was self-lacerating, it always culminated in self-justification through suffering. The laceration was purposeful and insincere. The whole corpus of his work might be entitled *The Passion and Apotheosis of August Strindberg as Directed by Himself.* It is always a dangerous critical practice to take an author at his valuation; and that is precisely what has produced the cultist tone of Strindbergian criticism, a good example of which is this passage by one of his translators:

> Despite a lessening of the awesome pessimism of Parts I and II, Part III lacks neither spirit nor drama. The theme follows, in substance, the same lines as in the first two dramas of the trilogy. The scenes in the home of the newlyweds and in the monastery have many fascinating and poetic nuances,

many delightful situations; and Strindberg's dialogue is ever brilliant and masterly. It is particularly stimulating in the scenes with the Tempter in Part III. Yet neither Part II nor Part III reaches the dramatic stature of Part I, whose grandeur and nobility place it in the vanguard of world dramas. The shifting scenes of futility and sanguinity, the fathomless imagination of the author juggling with occult and subliminal riddles, states of consciousness, and the awesome atmosphere engendered by the dramatist's gigantic genius for creating phantom worlds and characters of a dream life, set within the confines of the theatre, will be a lasting inspiration and a challenge not only to actors, stage directors, and producers, but, indeed, to all mankind. Repentance, remorse, and penance are the watchwords of Strindberg in this mighty drama.[6]

It is only the rare critic like Svanberg who can see through the self-preening insincerity of scenes such as that in which Strindberg, as The Stranger, pictures himself as having invented the Eighth Deadly Sin—Despair.[7]

The three plays entitled *To Damascus,* as well as *The Great Highway* (in which the Stranger is transformed into the Hunter and passes through seven stations on the highway of life), are usually seen as precursors of the German expressionist movement. Although I have treated them here principally as examples of conscious self-analysis, the fact that they confine the dramatic world to the boundaries of the author-protagonist's mind certainly does make them precursors of expressionism. In the third type of drama produced by Strindberg, however, the pre-expressionistic aspects are more definite. In *A Dream Play* and *The Ghost Sonata* the oneiric distortion of reality becomes the chief characteristic. Here the characters are not merely versions of aspects of the protagonist's character or beings created to illuminate aspects of the protagonist's self: they are purely emanations of the protagonist's mind. They are dreamed or imagined by him.

To anyone not familiar with the facts of Strindberg's personal life much of the three parts of *To Damascus* must seem incomprehensible. In order to understand those plays properly a preliminary reading of *Inferno* is practically mandatory; but even to those familiar with the life, as I have suggested already, the *To Damascus* plays must seem at best self-indulgent in the extreme, and an empathetic feeling for the protagonist must seem virtually impossible for one not afflicted with some of the same peculiarities. In *A Dream Play* Strindberg is, of course, still completely subjective. His is the mind of the Dreamer; and the Dreamer shares many of the Stranger's and the Hunter's psychological peculiarities. Nonetheless, *A Dream Play* is far more universal in its scope than the *To Damascus* plays. Strindberg is concerned here with the outer world's effect on the Dreamer and with his view of it. The significance for later drama is that the outer world is internalized and seen exclusively through the mind of the Dreamer. The Dreamer's mind twists and wrenches the world into a semblance of his own vision. Unless the play is to end in utter fantasy and madness, no solution can be presented, of course. As its title indicates, Strindberg's play consists entirely of the emanations of the mind of a central intelligence. The whole play is a realization of the Dreamer's stream of consciousness, and the play can be understood only if the reader or viewer identifies himself with this intelligence. The world is seen in the play as dreamt by the Daughter of Indra, who comes down to earth in order to understand the ways of men. Everything that happens in the play takes place in the boundless and amorphous realm of the dream. The daughter of the god comes to observe men and sees that they are unhappy and evil. Here, as in all expressionist drama, the atmosphere is pessimistic and angry, but there is an implicit belief in an undefined something that is better.

This is the essential difference between the social criticism of Ibsen the realist and Strindberg the expressionist. Both saw society as bad and in need of improvement, but whereas Ibsen and the realists dealt with specific evils of society and suggested specific ways of eliminating them, Strindberg and the expressionists bewailed the general evil of society and disseminated an evangelistic faith in a better world to come, without, however, holding out any specific hope. In *A Dream Play* Indra's

Daughter ascends again to heaven, having failed to solve anything. Evert Sprinchorn has identified three principal themes in *A Dream Play:* "The pitiableness of man's lot, the omnipotence of love, and the mystery of the universe."[8] The mystery of the universe remains unsolved, of course. It is supposedly concealed behind the door with the cloverleaf design on it. When the door is finally opened, nothing is seen behind it. Sprinchorn, I believe, misinterprets this event when he asserts that everything is behind it.[9] The whole point is that the meaning of everything is eternally enigmatic: nothing can ever be solved, nothing can ever be known, but the magnetic power of the search cannot be resisted. The door that attracts everybody, that promises everything and has nothing behind it, is one of Strindberg's more successful dramatic symbols, far more so than the childishly phallic castle tower with the chrysanthemum erupting from it with which the play ends. The themes of the pitiableness of mankind and the omnipotence of love are less subtle, but their importance, as well as that of the mystery of life, consists in their foreshadowing one of the principal themes of the expressionistic drama. Both thematically and technically *A Dream Play* is a remarkable pioneering work. Strindberg's own preface is worth quoting, for it could apply equally to any of the plays of the expressionists:

> . . . the author has in *A Dream Play* attempted to reproduce detached and disunited—although apparently logical— forms of dreams. Anything is apt to happen, anything seems possible and probable. Time and space do not exist. On a flimsy foundation of actual happenings, imagination spins and weaves in new patterns: an intermingling of remembrances, experiences, whims, fancies, ideas, fantastic absurdities and improvisations, and original inventions of the mind.
>
> The personalities split, take on duality, multiply, vanish, intensify, diffuse and disperse, and are brought into a focus. There is, however, one single-minded consciousness that exercises a dominance over the characters: the dreamer's. There are for the dreamer no secrets, no inconsequences, no scruples, no laws. He neither pronounces judgment nor exonerates; he merely narrates.

Since dreams most frequently are filled with pain, and less often with joy, a note of melancholy and a compassion for all living things runs through the limping story. Sleep, the liberator, often appears as a tormentor, a torturer, but when the agony is most oppressive the awakening rescues the sufferer and reconciles him to reality. No matter how agonizing reality may be, it will at this moment be welcomed cheerfully as a release from the painful dream.[10]

Strindberg's motives for writing in the expressionistic mode were personal—in the *To Damascus* plays he was psychologically motivated, in *A Dream Play* he was philosophically motivated. The German expressionists, who were active from about 1910 to about 1924, were socially motivated. Strindberg's personality—his inability to cope with the facts of his life, particularly his conjugal relations, and his inability to make sense of the outside world—led him to compress reality into his mind and eject it again molded by his inner vision. With the German expressionists it was different. Beyond the fact that they all felt rebellious toward their society it is difficult to glean any conception of their personalities from their works. Their plays were all distorted and violent visions of a society they hated. They were excoriations of a system they felt impotent to change and wanted to destroy.

Since Strindberg was strictly a forerunner of the expressionistic movement and did not share either its philosophical motives or its philosophical viewpoint (he did not, apparently, himself use the term; most authorities attribute its first use to the French painter Julien-Auguste Hervé in 1901), it might be as well to define it at this point. The clearest way to arrive at an understanding of the term is to contrast it with impressionism. Impressionism is an account of how the world of reality affects the describer. It is thus a subjective account of an objective perception. Expressionism, on the other hand, is an imposition on the outside world of the describer's conception of it. It is thus a subjective account of a subjective perception. Indeed, reality per se has no meaning for the expressionist. Everything in his art is "expressed," that is to say, brought forth from within himself. Expressionism is perhaps the most completely self-centered art form ever evolved. The expressionist writer takes the whole human race and the entire cosmos as his province, but he shows it to us as seen through the eyes of one character, invariably an alter ego for himself. Thus, for the expressionist the world is crammed into the compass of one man's vision, and, as it is completely subjective, it becomes deliberately and purposefully distorted. This subjective distortion always emerges in the form of protest and rebellion.

The expressionist movement was the symptom of a feeling of intense unrest and dissatisfaction among the younger generation of German writers in the second decade of the twentieth century. The German society that World War I destroyed had been a stifling and stultifying one based on a narrow-minded, patriarchal concept of the family with strongly pietistic overtones that, in the larger sphere, manifested itself in a rigid political authoritarianism. Thus, the protest and rebellion that we find in the expressionist drama is almost invariably directed against family relations and the way in which these relations prevent youth from developing its individuality. This twofold intention is the key to the purpose of the expressionist drama and explains the many seemingly outrageous scenes in which children castigate their parents (even to the point of killing or raping them) as well as the intense subjectivism that is an indirect way of asserting the writer-hero's individuality.

Intense subjectivism—the externalization of the writer's inner feelings—and an atmosphere of violence directed principally against the family as the basis of society are, then, the two chief characteristics of the expressionist drama. Only the author-hero is psychologically delineated. The other figures are usually puppetlike emanations of the protagonist's self-centered mind. Consequently, we find that the subsidiary characters in the expressionist drama are always types, virtually impersonal and frequently grotesque. The grotesquerie in the expressionist drama stems from the fact that the protagonist's view of people is invariably determined by his personal prejudices. These attitudes are always inimical to the other characters, who are usually either members of his own family or representatives of the authoritarian social order. As part of their criticism of these characters, the expressionists denied them psychological individuality and saw them only as marionettes jiggled around in a grotesque parody of existence through their unthinking devotion to the ideals of society. In many instances there is no attempt made to give the subsidiary characters any individuality but a symbolic one, and they then become abstractions that represent aspects of the state or society.

The first drama of the expressionist movement proper was Reinhard Sorge's *Der Bettler* (The Beggar). It was written in 1911 and published the following year, but it was not produced until 1917, a year after the playwright's death in battle. *Der Bettler* is an extremely significant beginning for the movement because it is not only the epitome of self-centered drama but also a plea for a new kind of theater. Sorge is himself the hero of his own drama, the plot of which concerns the Poet's efforts to find a theater willing to produce his play. This play, like Sorge's frame play, is intended for all humanity instead of for "a little heap of intellectuals." Sorge wishes to show mankind that it is inseparably linked to the Divine Mercy. His idea seems to be that what prevents mankind from perceiving this connection is the old patriarchal order. The Poet's father is depicted as insane, his mother as sick. The solution is the Poet's destruction of his parents. This theme of matricide and patricide was to appear either actually or symbolically in several other expressionist plays.

Sorge's early death prevented him from becoming an influential figure in the later development of the movement. This role was left to Walter Hasenclever, whose play *Der Sohn* (The Son, 1914) was the first play of the expressionist movement to be produced. Performed in Dresden in 1916, its success there was repeated in numerous theaters throughout Germany during the following years. Like *Der Bettler*, this drama was seminal in the development of expressionistic themes. The hero is a son rebelling against his father, who is depicted as being incapable of understanding the desires of youth and its strivings for freedom and self-realization. The son announces as his goal the destruction of the "medieval" tyranny of the family, which he calls a "witches' sabbath" and a "sulphurous torture chamber." We must, he says, "recreate freedom, mankind's highest good." The father locks the son up, but he escapes with a friend, and they attend a festival for the celebration of youth and joy. When the son has his final confrontation with the father, the latter threatens him with a whip, whereupon the son brandishes a revolver and the father dies of a stroke.

Hasenclever's other important play is *Die Menschen* (Humanity), which was produced in 1919. Here he specifies that the time is "Today" and the scene is "The World." The whole play is written in a series of disconnected, panoramic scenes shot through with a stichomythic, telegraphic dialogue. The story concerns a murdered man who rises from the grave carrying a sack with his head in it. He then embarks on a wild career of gambling and drinking during which he associates with madmen, prostitutes, alcoholics, and degenerates of all types. Finally, he is himself sentenced as his own murderer and returns to his grave. Hasenclever was perhaps the most self-centered writer of a movement in which that quality was the keynote. As one of his characters says, "Can't you understand? You can only live in a state of ecstasy; reality would only hamper you. How wonderful it is always to realize that you are the most important person in the whole world!"

Oskar Kokoschka is justly celebrated more as a painter than as a dramatist, but his contributions cannot be ignored in a survey of expressionist drama. *Mörder, Hoffnung der Frauen (Murderer, Hope of Women)* was premiered in Dresden in 1916, although it had been written several years earlier and performed by Kokoschka's friends and associates in Vienna. In Kokoschka's work the struggle for a new apocalyptic freedom is translated into a struggle between the sexes. The father-son opposition of Sorge and Hasenclever becomes a man-woman opposition, so that Kokoschka is more closely related to Wedekind as far as his thematic material is concerned.

The expressionist dramatists were not, as has been frequently supposed, essentially products of the First World War. The confusion has arisen from the natural association of writers of protest with antiwar plays. It is true that the majority of the expressionists did not approve of the war, but the type of specific protest that an antiwar play demanded was opposed to their deepest feelings. They were more at home in vague, generalized protests against the nature of society and the family than in a particular dissent against the war. The only successful play concerning the war that any of the expressionists produced was Reinhard Goering's *Seeschlacht* (Naval Battle), produced in 1918. This play, however, is not an example of pure expressionism. Goering uses the language of expressionism, but he does not use the single-viewpoint technique. Instead, there are seven subjective viewpoints—those of the seven sailors trapped in a gun turret aboard a German battleship just before the battle of Jutland. They are all nameless types representing various human attitudes. One of the sailors decides to start a mutiny and sacrifice himself for a higher idea than the Fatherland: the freedom of his comrades. Before he can organize the mutiny, however, the battle begins, and he fights alongside his comrades. The play ends on an ambiguous note as one of the two surviving sailors says that the battle is still raging on. Since the speaker is the sailor who had contemplated mutiny, his remark might refer to the war for the Fatherland or the struggle for ultimate freedom.

The other prominent expressionist dramatist who dealt with the war was Fritz von Unruh. The son of a general, von Unruh is best known for his expressionist trilogy about war in the abstract: *Ein Geschlecht* (A Race of Men), performed in 1917, *Platz* (Place), produced in 1920, and *Dietrich*. The last play was not written until 1936, when von Unruh was in exile in France, and thus does not belong to the expressionist movement. In *Ein Geschlecht* von Unruh deals with the fate of a mother, four sons, and a daughter. He specifies that the time is anytime, and the place is a cemetery on a mountaintop. The Mother, the Daughter, and the Youngest Son are burying another son, who has fallen in battle. Meanwhile, the other two sons are brought up to the cemetery from the valley below, where a battle is going on. The soldiers who bring them say that the Youngest Son must redeem his race by executing his two brothers, who have been sentenced to death—one for committing atrocities, the other for cowardice. When the Youngest Son refuses to do his "duty," he is dragged away to the battlefield. The two themes of the play, both typically expressionistic, are the guilt of the Mother for bringing her sons into the world and the birth of a "new age," which will come about when the world is cleansed of its sins through the revolution that the Youngest Son prepares to lead at the end of the play. The second play, *Platz,* is a fantastically confused account of the Youngest Son's leadership of the revolution. Von Unruh's importance rests in his attempt to carry the themes of expressionism to their extreme, but the incoherence of his language, which is more marked than that of the other members of the movement, prevents his plays from having any lasting significance.

Paul Kornfeld was an extremely important theorist of expressionism. It was he who coined the term "Seelendrama" (drama of the soul) when he proclaimed, "Let us leave character to the everyday world, and let us be nothing but soul . . . for the soul pertains to Heaven, while character is earthbound. . . . Psychology tells us as little about man as anatomy does." Kornfeld thus disposes of the traditional dramatic elements of characterization and motivation. In 1917 his most significant expressionist drama was produced: *Die Verführung* (The Seduction), another of the plays in which the author-hero (here significantly named Bitterlich) seeks the meaning of life and announces an apocalyptic vision of humanity.

Expressionism was a movement that attracted many German authors of the time. In addition to the playwrights already mentioned, whose most important work was expressionist, there were others, such as Ernst Toller, Carl Sternheim, Georg Kaiser, Franz Werfel, Yvan Goll, and Ernst Barlach, who experimented briefly with expressionism but whose principal literary achievements were elsewhere. The influence of expressionism outside Germany, however, was minimal. It seems to have been a way of thinking peculiarly fitted to the ethos of the German thinkers at that particular time. Such influence as it has had outside Germany has been limited to adaptations of expressionist style rather than philosophy.

The only prominent expressionist playwright of the post–World War II period in Germany was the brilliant Wolfgang Borchert, whose *Draussen vor der Tür* (The Outsider) is one of the most powerful and one of the best of all expressionist plays. Borchert had precisely the same reason for writing as the World War I German expressionists did: disillusionment with society and a feeling of disgust and horror at the effects of war. Borchert's reaction to postwar Germany is, like that of his predecessors, an anguished and frustrated scream. He uses the theme of the soldier returned from the war to find everything reduced to rubble and ruins. In two magnificent satiric scenes, entirely expressionist in technique, he exposes the German's love of militarism and his ability to anesthetize his moral sense. In one scene, Beckmann, the returned soldier, goes to visit the colonel of his old regiment. Beckmann has been having nightmares because the colonel once made him responsible for a group of men, eleven of whom were killed. In this nightmare, which is always the same, Beckmann is haunted by the eleven women the soldiers had left behind and by a giant skeletal figure in a general's uniform that plays on an enormous xylophone made of human bones. As Beckmann relates the dream to the colonel, he becomes more and more hysterical; the sound of the frantic xylophone fills the theater, and the colonel turns into the nightmarish figure of the skeleton in the dream. The other scene is very simple. Beckmann has stolen a bottle of liquor from the colonel's table, and in his drunkenness he savagely caricatures the army routines that in his youth had enslaved his mind and crippled his body. Almost beside himself with rage, Beckmann struts around the stage in a grotesque parody of the goose step, shouting "Heil!" at every step. Borchert could not have written a sharper denunciation of the Nazi ritual than this furious, twisted ridicule. The most interesting aspect of Borchert's revival of the expressionist technique is the change that has taken place in the object of the rebellion. The battle against the family as a symbol of repression has now been won—indeed, has become out of date. The post–World War II expressionist does not write plays about sons struggling against fathers; he faces the conflict directly and writes of sons struggling against their country and against God.

Borchert was essentially an anachronism: he was writing expressionist drama at a time when that style had long since been abandoned. By 1945 the individual vision had become of secondary importance—some might say of no importance. The highly egoistic assumption of Strindberg and of the expressionists that the confusion of the world could be controlled by being compressed into their minds and reimagined there had been replaced by the more objective and more nihilistic attitude for which the work of Alfred Jarry was as seminal as Strindberg's was for expressionism.

But before we deal with the theater that emanated from Jarry, there is one other figure that has interesting affinities with Strindberg and the expressionists; and that is Luigi Pirandello. Pirandello came to a consideration of life as subjective experience by a quite different path from that hacked out by Strindberg. Strindberg's own madness and his inability to explain or cope with the world caused him to withdraw into himself and make his mind the world. The expressionists' perception of the madness of the world around them, the illogic and injustice of the society they grew up in, caused them to withdraw into themselves and re-form the world into a parental ogre that had to be destroyed in the inevitable generational conflict. This had the theatrical disadvantage of being a self-perpetuating "solution" to an ever-recurring problem, which is the basic reason for the ephemeral nature of their movement. I. B. Singer neatly took care of the expressionist philosophy in a lecture once by remarking that the present generational conflict would inevitably solve itself within the next forty years.

Pirandello came to philosophical subjectivism through a perception of his wife's madness. In 1903, as a result of the shock caused by the news of the loss of the family fortune in a mine disaster, Pirandello's wife lost her sanity, i.e., her grasp on reality. This event occurred after nine years of marriage and three children, and manifested itself in an extreme paranoid condition, the outward sign of which was an unreasoning and unreasonable jealousy. Pirandello put up with this for sixteen years before putting his wife in a nursing home, where she remained for forty years until her death in 1959. One cannot help wondering whether Pirandello put up with her for sixteen years because of financial exigency, because of compassion, because of a desire to maintain some semblance of family life for the children, or because of purposes of clinical observation. Certainly the observation of his wife's behavior enabled Pirandello to develop his theory of subjective reality. What was evident to him was that his wife's jealous tantrums were without factual basis; what was equally evident to him was that his wife was absolutely convinced of the truth of her suspicions. It followed that there were here two equally believed "truths." If two people could have diametrically opposed conceptions of the "truth" of a matter, it followed that three people could have three, and so on ad infinitum. The number of subjective viewpoints on any particular situation, however minimally they may differ, is limited only by the number of people considering the situation, and, theoretically, by the number of people alive. Objective truth is, therefore, a meaningless concept. In Strindberg and the expressionists, for different reasons, the world is encompassed in the mind of the manipulating individual; in Pirandello the world is separately encompassed in the mind of each separate individual. There are as many "truths" as there are thinkers, and these "truths" are and must by their very nature remain mutually incommunicable, each individual mind being like a separate enclosed monad. For Pirandello "reality never exists in itself."[11] It exists created anew in each mind. The situation in his own family gave Pirandello the viewpoint that only the subjective life exists, that each person has his own reality. This led him from Strindberg's pure subjectivism to subjective relativism, a humanistic transformation since it recognizes and respects the existence of others; but, nevertheless, still a rejection of objective reality and therefore of the possibility of its manipulation. Pirandello's work represents a development of Strindberg's but not a radical departure from it.

Pirandello's place in fragmentational drama is clear in that his belief in a different reality within every mind implies a belief in an incomprehensible and unmanageable world. He has been aptly described as "the writer in whose work all former ties and points of reference in the life of man will become devoid of meaning and the inconsequence of chaos will seem to be the sole law and sensible expedient."[12] The absence of all former ties and points of reference in the life of man alludes, of course, to the discrediting of religion as a viable explanation of the world, leaving only the "inconsequence of chaos." Pirandello, like Strindberg and the expressionists, reacted by withdrawing into the mind. The only difference is that being socially oriented instead of self-absorbed, he let others withdraw into their own minds instead of postulating his own mind as the supreme consciousness. The difference between his concept of truth and that of writers who believe in the reality of objective truth can perhaps best be explained by the images of the crystal and the Chinese boxes. For the objectivists truth is like a set of Chinese boxes. One opens the first box and finds another box inside it; one opens that one and finds another; one opens that one and finds another. And so on and so on and so on. Until finally one comes upon a tiny box, too small to hold another box, too small to hold anything but the core of the puzzle, the infinitesimally minute and infinitely valuable grain of truth. One must only persevere, work hard enough, indefatigably open up enough boxes, follow out a sufficiently long sequence of logical clues—and the solution to the problem will be discovered. For Pirandello the Chinese-box image of truth was invalid. He imagined truth as a crystal with an infinite number of facets. In such a crystal each facet would be equal in area and would reflect an equal amount of light—but each facet would reflect its light in a slightly different direction. No facet could be said to reflect light more clearly than any other. Each facet (human being) has its own "truth."

Pirandello's subjective relativism seems to be an extremely humanistic philosophy with its uncompromising respect for every conceivable viewpoint. But there can be no denying that it is a retreat from reality. A myriad of realities, all equally valid, is effectively the same as no reality at all. In the final analysis Pirandello arrives at the same point of stasis as Strindberg does: to recognize an infinity of subjective realities is no better than to recognize only one's own. It is merely less rigid, more accommodating. A philosophy founded on a recognition of the existential validity of dementia must inevitably itself become demented. For Pirandello to acknowledge that his wife's paranoid delusions were sincerely held and constituted an objective reality for her is indicative of his humane understanding; for him to grant them equal validity with his own perceptions is to postulate universal paranoia. By accepting his wife's delusions at her own valuation he did violence to what he *knew* to be objective, discoverable reality. Pirandello's wife was absolutely and sincerely convinced that he was constantly unfaithful to her. That he was not is a fact that he *knew* to be true. By giving equal validity to all points of view he was thus denying the existence of discoverable fact, rejecting the outer world as hopelessly chaotic and retreating into his own mind. "Truth" became something purely personal, closed off, hermetic—exactly as in Strindberg. If we accept Camus' definition of insanity as loss of consciousness of self—and I can think of no better definition—then Pirandello's acceptance of the validity of a consciousness of self that is in direct contradiction of observable, verifiable fact constitutes a denial of the state of insanity: "sanity" and "insanity" become synonyms.

Pirandello is best known and most admired for those plays, particularly *Six Characters in Search of an Author*, in which he attempts to probe the borders of art and reality. These plays become complex indeed in their implications and are best considered after the plays that examine appearance and reality, the most prominent of which are *Right You Are, If You Think You Are* and *Henry IV*. These plays, furthermore, best exemplify Pirandello's central theory, discussed above, of multiple realities. The plot of *Right You Are* concerns the identity of Sra. Ponza. Her husband has just moved into town to assume an official position. The local society invites him to parties, but he always comes alone. Not only does Ponza not bring his wife to parties, he does not even allow her out of the house. Naturally, gossip is rife and speculation abounds, fed by the information that not even Ponza's mother-in-law is permitted to visit her. Ponza's explanation of this bizarre situation is that his first wife, the mother-in-law's daughter, is dead and he has remarried. But in order to spare the old lady, who has deluded herself into believing that her daughter is still alive, he continues the fiction of being married to his first wife and permits the old lady to see her only from afar. Sra. Frola, the mother-in-law, has an entirely different version of the matter. According to her, Ponza is suffering from the delusion that her daughter has been killed and that he has remarried. She and her daughter encourage this delusion at great cost to themselves lest he go off the deep end altogether. Both versions explain the circumstances equally well. Only one can be true, though of course both could be false. At the climax of the play the wife appears, heavily veiled, at a gathering of the most prominent townspeople, whose scandalmongering curiosity has forced Ponza to agree to produce his wife in public. Nothing is resolved and the issue is left hanging as the wife announces that she is both Ponza's second wife, as he claims, and the old lady's daughter, as she asserts. "For myself," the wife says, "I am nobody. . . . I am she whom you believe me to be." The play ends on this note of irresolution.

There are several possible ways of interpreting this play. As a satire of hypocritical social busybodies it is perfect. Strictly speaking, it is none of the town's business what Ponza does in his private family life. He could be telling the truth; his mother-in-law (if she *is* his mother-in-law) could be telling the truth; they could both be suffering from delusions, and the wife could be humoring both of them; the wife could be schizoid, believing that she is both Ponza's second wife and Sra. Frola's daughter; or she could be Ponza's mistress pretending to be Sra. Frola's daughter. Other permutations are no doubt possible. The mastery of the play as social satire consists in the fact that the audience is seduced into wondering what the truth of the matter is just as much as the repellent and prying townspeople are; and are left hanging just as much at the end. The inconclusive ending in effect tells it that it is none of its business. Pirandello has succeeded here in writing audience-participation drama on a much higher level of sense than in his later more direct and more jejune experiments in that area with such plays as *Each in His Own Way*. If, however, the play be interpreted as an exposition of Pirandello's ideas about the subjective relativity of truth, it takes on a different aspect altogether. In that case we are asked to believe that the truth, instead of being nobody's business but that of the individuals concerned, is undiscoverable. Thus, just as Pirandello's wife sincerely believed that she was the victim of a diabolically clever Don Juan, so Ponza really believes that his first wife is dead and that he has remarried; Sra. Frola really believes that Ponza is mentally ill and is still married to his first wife, her daughter; and Sra. Ponza really believes that she is nobody at all while being at the same time her husband's second wife *and* Sra. Frola's daughter. And all of these "truths" have equal validity. Qua philosophy, this is nonsense. Given the situation of the play, *one* of the possibilities is factually true. Either Ponza's wife is his first or his second (or she is someone else), and either she is or she is not the old lady's daughter. Each believes in his own vision, but one of these visions is objectively factual—and which one it is could be verified. Each viewpoint on the same reality may be supremely true for the individual observer, but one viewpoint *is* true. To argue as Pirandello does is to argue for the *objective* validity of hallucinations. In fact Pirandello would agree that hallucinations have only subjective validity, but he would argue that there is no such thing as objective validity, thus aligning himself with Strindberg and the expressionists. Recognizing that the outside world is senseless, that "the inconsequence of chaos . . . [is] . . . the sole law and sensible expedient," Pirandello takes this to its logical conclusion by rejecting *all* manifestations of the outside world. A clear case of cavalierly pouring out the baby with the bath water.

In *Henry IV* Pirandello is doing much the same thing, though in a theatrically more sophisticated way. In the earlier play Pirandello had written about the relativity of social appearances; in *Henry IV* he wrote about the relativity of character. In the revised version of *Six Characters in Search of an Author*

Pirandello specified that the six characters should wear actual masks indicative of the principal motivation of each character (a mask showing "revenge" for the Stepdaughter, for example). There is some doubt whether he literally intended the play to be presented in this way, and in fact it never is; nevertheless, the instruction is significant in that it demonstrates Pirandello's fundamental view of the nature of human character. The six characters wear masks to indicate that they are immutable because they are artifacts and not human beings; the human beings (the actors who rehearse the play) do not wear masks because their personalities are kaleidoscopic and multifaceted. In *Henry IV* we see this multifaceted quality of the human personality demonstrated, although only in the person of the protagonist. This is a play in which the attention is totally concentrated on the main character, all the others rotating round him like satellites around a star. The protagonist is an upper-class Italian who, twenty years before the opening of the play, acted the part of the German emperor Henry IV in a pageant. As the result of falling off his horse, thanks to the interference of his rival for the hand of Matilda, he became convinced that he *was* Henry IV. In order to protect him, his rich family has humored this delusion for twenty years, hiring people to form a mini-court around him with eleventh-century costumes and constant discussions of papal-imperial politics as gleaned from a cursory reading of history books (the eleventh-century "realism" does not have to be very profound since there is no reason to assume that the protagonist was a historical scholar before he fell off his horse). Unbeknownst to anyone but himself, "Henry IV" recovered his sanity spontaneously after twelve years. For the last eight, therefore, he has deliberately been living a masquerade: everyone has supposed him still to be suffering from the insane delusion (real and factual to him) that he is Henry IV of Germany, and only he has known that he has returned to his original personality. His explanation for continuing the masquerade is that when he came to himself he realized that he had missed the best part of his life and that he would feel ridiculous if he were to go back now to the banquet table of life at which everyone else of his generation had already feasted, as he puts it. The action of the play takes place in a few hours and consists in an attempt to bring Henry back to "sanity." Matilda, now the mistress of Belcredi, Henry's former rival who engineered his fall from the horse, brings along her daughter, who looks very much as she herself did twenty years ago when Henry loved her. It is the opinion of a doctor she has hired, surely one of the least intelligent physicians in literature, that the shock of suddenly seeing the daughter will bring the patient back to himself. Instead, the "patient" is infuriated at the transparent cruelty of the proposed trick and vents his rage by fatally stabbing Belcredi. This, of course, condemns him to playing the part of an insane man for the rest of his life to avoid arrest and condemns the others to a conspiracy of silence. The point of all this is the constantly shifting realities of Henry's personality. For the first twelve years after his fall off the horse he seemed to be mad to everyone, but did not seem so to himself. He was absolutely and sincerely convinced of the reality of his vision of himself as the Emperor Henry IV, just as Pirandello observed that his wife was absolutely and sincerely convinced of the reality of *her* delusive visions. In other words, during those twelve years when Henry said he was the emperor of Germany he was speaking the literal truth, just as the people around him were speaking the literal truth when they said he was not. For the next eight years Henry was sane and knew perfectly well who he was (i.e., who he had been before the accident), but since he continued to *pretend* to be Henry IV he continued to *appear* to be insane to those around him. Previously Henry IV knew he was Henry IV and the others knew he was not. Now Henry IV knows he is not Henry IV but pretends that he is while the others continue exactly as before. With the killing of Belcredi the masks become four: Henry IV knows he is not Henry IV but must continue to pretend that he is; the others still know that he is not, but must now begin in earnest to pretend that he is.

As an example of fragmentational drama *Henry IV* is outstanding. Pirandello shows his view that reality is something that can be seen only from within and is transformed—truly transformed, for one man's vision is as good as another's—into a new aspect by each individual observer. As an example of theatrical drama *Henry IV* suffers from an extremely awkward and transparently contrived plot. Critics have argued that Pirandello deliberately wrote conventional melodramatic plots so that the story line would not distract the audience and would enable it instead to concentrate its attention on the play's philosophical context. A sort of pre-Brechtian Italian version of the alienation technique, in fact. In the event, however, this does not work in performance, and the melodramatic plots tend instead to distract and irritate or to absorb the members of the audience, depending on their tastes in these matters. A more likely, if less flattering, explanation of the triteness of Pirandello's plots is that he partook of the universal tendency of Italian playwrights up to his time to be essentially misplaced opera librettists.

Withdrawal from the world as a philosophical viewpoint becomes even more pronounced in Pirandello's *Six Characters in Search of an Author* and *Each in His Own Way*. *Six Characters* has become one of the most explicated plays of the modern theater, and it has remained one of the most puzzling. Explication has usually taken the form of complex disquisitions on the nature of stage illusion and illusive "reality" and on the comparative sincerity of emotion in "real" people and in created characters. I would like to suggest here that the air around the play needs to be cleared, that it is not profound at all, and that it is another example of the theme on which Pirandello figured so many variations: a statement of despair in the face of a world in which truth is infinitely multifaceted and a desperate retreat into a self-created fantasy world. The explications of *Six Characters* are understandable: the play *does* have the appearance of profundity. But the key word there is *appearance*, which is, indeed, so constant a preoccupation of Pirandello's. The profundity of *Six Characters* is like the *apparent* profundity that one sees in a pair of opposed mirrors: when one looks into them one sees an infinitely regressing series of images. But the regression into depth is an illusion: the images are in fact all on the same plane.

One of the confusing aspects of *Six Characters* has always been the imperfection of the story the six intruders bring onto the stage. In the frame play a rehearsal of one of Pirandello's other plays is going on (an amusing bit of "in" humor at the same time that it is a subtle intensification of the mirror effect) when suddenly six peculiar-looking people materialize as if coagulating out of thin air. In effect that is precisely what they do, for they claim to be the unfinished creations of a playwright's mind condemned to act out the events of their story forever. They try to persuade the actors to give them life by acting their story, but find that their "lives" become even less convincing in the hands of these ever-changing merchants of artificiality. Albert Bermel has subjected the plot of the play within the play to a minute textual scrutiny and has come up with a brilliant explication of the story of the six characters.[13] Briefly, Bermel argues convincingly that the family relationships Pirandello gives us are deliberately misleading: the Son is actually the Father's stepson, the Stepdaughter his real daughter, and the Little Girl the result of an incestuous affair between the Father and the (Step)daughter. Bermel's theory is a superb piece of textual detective work, but it is based on what I believe to be a wholly mistaken approach to literature. Bermel makes Pirandello's assumption—that the characters have a life of their own, and that this is worth analyzing (i.e., the characters are treated as living human beings). This approach may have a certain usefulness for the actor studying the role (although, speaking as an actor, I would tend to doubt even this), but as literary criticism it represents precisely that retreat into a fantasized reality characteristic of the fragmentational dramatists. Elsewhere in his book Bermel excoriates thematic criticism and even goes so far as to proclaim that it is dead.[14] But he makes the mistake of treating theater as a reality rather than as the reflection of a reality. Popular theater is a reflection of current tastes, mores, and prejudices; intellectual theater is a reflection of current philosophical and political trends. To examine theater from any other point of view is to relegate it by implication to the status of a fairy tale—not to myth, which is quite a different thing altogether—or, in other words, to the level of escape literature. Looked at from any other point of view but the thematic, theater is no more significant than a detective story, a rubber of bridge, or a football game.

Although Bermel's analysis of the inner plot of *Six Characters* is probably correct in the sense that he has almost certainly divined Pirandello's intentions, the play becomes no more meaningful as a result of it. Close textual analysis is of no particular use in performance since there is no obvious way of getting the point across to the audience. Even if it were possible, the play would not thus be made more meaningful since it would still remain facile melodrama and nothing more. If the inner play of the six characters were written out fully in accordance with Bermel's analysis, it might at best become a study of a unique case of psychopathy in the figure of the Father. But Pirandello deliberately refrained from completing the inner plot as if to point up the fact that the plot was not the object on which he wanted the audience to concentrate its attention. What he wanted the audience to concentrate its attention on was the contrast between the six characters he created *as* characters and the other characters (the Director, the actors, and the technical staff) that he created as "real people." These latter partake of the defect that Pirandello saw in himself and in every human being around him: they are multifaceted and dynamic personalities, constantly changing, incapable of being "formulated . . . [and] pinned . . . on the wall." The six characters, on the other hand, have only the minds and personalities their creator has given them *and they cannot change these.* They are what real people would be if the world were not a seething chaos. Pirandello's thesis is that the creations of the artist are more "real" than real people because they do not change, because they can be defined once and for all. For him art was a nostalgic refuge from a world that did not make sense.

There is another, more complex aspect to the play that comes out even more clearly in *Each in His Own Way.* Pirandello is rightly considered to be a radical innovator in theatrical technique, and his theories have had an enormous—and, I believe, unfortunate—influence on subsequent playwrights and directors. As a result of his theory that the created static characters have more inherent reality than the accidental dynamic human beings, Pirandello evolved a presentational technique that attempted to break down the barriers between the staged situation and the audience. He did this by trying to convince the audience that what was taking place on the stage was "really" taking place rather than being merely conventional pretense. One might explain this by borrowing a term from metaphysical poetry and saying that he was trying to make a conceit concrete. The conceit was that there were no actors on the stage but real human beings undergoing real situations. Given the conditions of the theatrical form, which Pirandello willfully ignored, this is manifestly self-contradictory. Thus, in *Six Characters* the characters in the frame story—the actors, the Director, and the technical staff—are intended to be looked upon not as actors playing actors, etc., but as real people who happen to be actors by profession going through a real rehearsal on which the audience happens to drop in. What appears to be a play within a play was for Pirandello a play (the story of the six characters) within an actual rehearsal. The conceit further supposes that the six characters are not played by actors but *are themselves*.

His intentions in this matter of ignoring the traditional concept of theater can be seen more clearly in *Each in His Own Way*. In this play Pirandello's conceit is that reality and pretense cannot be distinguished from each other. He attempts to demonstrate this thesis by carrying the play not only off the stage and into the theater itself but out into the street as well. What he does here, it should be noted, is not at all the same as what has come to be known as "street theater." The latter is the act of frankly putting on a theatrical performance in the street and is an evocation of a tradition far older than Pirandello's theater—that of the commedia dell'arte. The simplest form of theater is the street-theater–commedia structure of two barrels and a plank; the simplest form of theatrical performance consists of an interaction between two people, one openly pretending to be someone else and one watching him. Pirandello had neither of these in mind when he wrote *Each in His Own Way*. His theater was the conventional theater but he had it spill out into the street; his form of theatrical performance consisted in having the actors embark on the inevitably vain attempt to conceal the fact that they are pretending. The play purports to be a *drame à clef*, the action being based on a scandal that is actually taking place in real life. To reinforce this impression Pirandello specifies that an actor playing a newsboy hawks specially printed papers, in which the details of the scandal are described, on the street outside the theater. Other actors playing the parts of these "real" people stage an altercation in the lobby of the theater before the play and during the intermission. Their protests at the thinly disguised reproduction of their affair on the stage cause the last act to be canceled.

It is difficult to see what Pirandello intended by this if he did not intend the audience to feel that they were at a theatrical performance broken up by "reality"—that the people in the audience and in the lobby were not actors at all but real people really appalled at seeing their personal situations dramatized on the stage. Yet such an illusion is manifestly impossible except perhaps at the first performance. What he probably intended was a melding of the lines dividing the theater from reality: art imitating life and vice versa in equal proportion. Unfortunately, in attempting to do this, he ignored *the* fundamental principal of theater: a frankly asserted artificiality. Art is not and cannot be life: it is and must be a purposefully distorted reflection of life. Pirandello made the mistake of willfully ignoring Coleridge's dictum of the audience's automatic suspension of disbelief. Theater is quintessentially artificial, but the psychological force that it exerts through its ambience causes an automatic and tacit pact to be formed instinctively between audience and actors. Pirandello failed to recognize the existence of this pact. His theatrical technique is an attempt to create the pact by trying to involve the audience in the action and to eliminate the atmosphere of artificiality that he felt was inappropriate. But the attempt to create what is already there has the paradoxical effect of destroying it. With actors planted in the audience, the audience automatically regains its disbelief and the necessary illusion by which theater lives and breathes is shattered. Pirandello is a conjurer who lets his audience see him put the rabbit in the hat before pulling it out again. The resulting flourish inevitably falls flat. In *Each in His Own Way* he does this from the point of view of the plot; in *Tonight We Improvise* from the point of view of the actor. The actress who is improvising the leading role of Mommina becomes so emotionally involved in what she is doing that she is personally affected: while playing a death scene she almost dies herself. But of course the actress is playing an actress who almost dies while playing a death scene; and ending the play at this point on the grounds that the actress is *really* incapacitated is the extremity of spuriousness.

Quite apart from the criticism that can justifiably be made of Pirandello's misunderstanding of the essential nature of theater, his innovations in theatrical technique must be seen as an attempt to render his theories on the relativity of truth and the consequent unknowability of reality into concrete form. Seen from this point of view Pirandello's "theater" plays—*Six Characters, Each in His Own Way,* and *Tonight We Improvise*—are powerful, if essentially untheatrical, statements of that rejection of the outside world and withdrawal into the cocoon of the mind that motivated Strindberg and the expressionists.[15]

The anarchic and chaotic view of the world that I have characterized in the theater as fragmentational drama exists in two forms. Strindberg, the expressionists, and Pirandello exemplify one of the natural reactions to a world that has ceased to make sense, that is no longer believed to be operating in accordance with a rule book interpreted by ever-helpful infallible guides. They retreated into the self and formed their own unique and individualistic conceptions of the world there or, as was the case with Pirandello in his "theater" plays, they sought refuge in a frankly artificial world and tried to impose the concept of artefact as reality on the chaotic outside world. By postulating that reality consisted of the frozen timelessness of art Pirandello attempted to impose order and meaning on the random chaos of reality.

The other form of this *Weltanschauung* sprang from the work of Alfred Jarry. Here there was no internalizing. The meaninglessness and chaos of reality were recognized, accepted—and attacked. E. F. Benson defined this attitude neatly if unsympathetically when he said, "The whole history of the progress of Art is, necessarily, a history of revolts against conventions, but the rebels . . . are of two classes. One of these consists of hooligans whose delight is merely in smashing but who have nothing else to offer in place of what they consider worthless. The other class is of those whose iconoclasm makes room for something worthier, which they profess themselves ready to supply."[16]

Jarry was the original "hooligan." Benson was writing of Victorian rebels, and his "other class" with something worthier to supply were the Pre-Raphaelites. For him hooliganism was the worst kind of artistic pejorative. Jarry, however, raised artistic hooliganism to the status of a philosophy that has prevailed in one form or another down to the present day. This may be deplorable, but it can be deplored only by critics prone to wishful and nostalgic thinking. Hooliganism may be defined as contempt for and destruction of the visible images of the existing order. Social and political hooliganism may be deplorable; artistic hooliganism may not. The latter is a re-sponse to and reflection of the former. Jarry's artistic hooligan-ism shocked his contemporaries because it reflected something that he had instinctively perceived with his artist's prophetic vision, but which nobody else had yet noticed, or, having noticed, was willing to admit: that the old order, the carefully dovetailed structure of society based on the imagined founda-tion of religion, lay shattered in randomly strewn bits and pieces with no trace remaining of the finely honed jointures that had held them together for so long against all reason and common sense. Nor were reason and common sense able to put them together again. Jarry and his followers saw the social order as a monstrous Humpty-Dumpty that had perched pre-cariously on its wall of faith for so long, issuing arbitrary proclamations about the meaning of meaning. It had finally fallen off—or, rather, the wall had been shown never to have been there at all—and the fragile shards were being crushed even more irrevocably by those who were desperately trying to paste them together and levitate them again. This view is

superbly illustrated in a short play, *Le jet de sang* (The Jet of
Blood), by Jarry's chief interpreter, Antonin Artaud. In a stage
direction Artaud has two stars crashing together (the ineluctable, random, and incomprehensible cosmic forces), and as a
result a jumble of parts of human bodies and man-made artefacts (colonnades, porches, temples, and alembics) fall from
above, rapidly at first, then ever more slowly, as if the laws of
physics were themselves uncertain. Finally three scorpions, a
frog, and a beetle float down. The cascade of bits and pieces of
human scientific and cultural achievements gradually negat-
ing the theory of gravity is followed, as if they were an ironic
exclamation mark commenting on the meaninglessness of human progress, by the three primeval creatures that have maintained themselves unchanged since before man or mammal
evolved. The negation of the theory of gravity is symbolic of
the chaos that is immanent in human affairs: there is no hook
to hold onto; everything floats free on random paths. Despite
all the evidence of history, despite all the accomplishments of
the intellect, we are back to—have never, indeed, emerged
from—a world in which the scorpion and the beetle reign
supreme and the frog croaks mindlessly from the primeval
slime. A little later in this short play the collapse of Humpty-
Dumpty's wall is made even more explicit in another stage
direction:

> Night suddenly falls. Earthquake. Thunder shakes the air
> and lightning zigzags in all directions. In the intermittent
> flashes of lightning one sees people running around in
> panic, embracing each other, falling down, getting up again,
> and running around like madmen. At a given moment an
> enormous hand seizes The Whore's hair, which bursts into
> ever-widening flames.[17]

The hand is God's, and the Whore bites it, releasing an im-
mense jet of blood. The wall of faith has here become frankly
the plaything of satire, made all the more mordant and vicious
by disappointment. The Whore's hair bursts into an aureole of
flame, a cruel mockery of the glory that haloed the saints, while
the bloody jet that spurts forth when the Whore bites into

God's flesh reduces the sacrament of the Eucharist to an act of instinctive feral savagery—an act of revenge, as it were, for centuries of enslavement to an empty ceremony.

Jarry's Ubu is the artistic avatar of this attitude to life.[18] In Jarry's Ubu plays—*Ubu roi, Ubu cocu,* and *Ubu enchaîné* (Ubu the King, Ubu Cuckolded, Ubu in Chains)—the fantastic, grotesque figure of Ubu is a symbol of the negation of traditional morality and of the disembodied, mindless, and incomprehensible forces that crush men like a juggernaut, driving them without discernible reason to the ultimate senselessness and degradation of death. Ubu embodies these forces, but perhaps—indeed, probably—they do not exist. Ubu is a dramatically and philosophically necessary materialization of the Void, of that vacuum in which chaos reigns as the human monads drift and zoom in haphazard paths, colliding sometimes fatally, bouncing off each other into equally causeless trajectories, melding momentarily into illusory union only to be ripped apart again to resume their aimless courses until they sputter out, dissolve, and are forgotten. And are as if they had never been. Ubu also represents the animal instinct in every person: the primal id that refuses to remain suppressed. On the social scale he personifies the outbursts of bestiality caused by the barbaric and elemental destructive instinct in the human soul that Freud believed was ineradicable and that caused his denial of the supremacy of culture over the instincts.[19]

Jarry was misunderstood during his lifetime, although he himself was probably not aware of the full import of his nightmarish vision. A few people, William Butler Yeats among them, sensed the sinister aspect lurking behind the clown mask of Ubu. Yeats was present at the riotous premiere on December 10, 1896, and commented succinctly, "After us, the Savage God."[20] The Savage God, indeed. No longer a benevolent God floating gracefully across the ceiling of the Sistine Chapel caressing life into man with gentle fingertips, but a formless Fury frenziedly hurling thunderbolts at man. Strindberg and his followers reacted by huddling into themselves; Jarry and his followers by glorying in the self and with cynical mockery defying that which crushed them inexorably.

The Jarryesque manner can be seen most clearly in two intellectual attitudes that have become quite well known though widely misunderstood. One of these is Jarry's invention of the pseudoscience of 'Pataphysics; the other is Antonin Artaud's development of the concept of the theater of cruelty. The latter, besides being merely misunderstood, has also been subjected to widespread misinterpretation with disastrous results for subsequent theatrical productions.[21]

Like so much that Jarry created, whether written or lived (for Jarry's life was itself a deliberately created work of art, an animated philosophical novel), 'Pataphysics seems at first glance to be a macabre joke—an early example of what has come to be known as black humor. But the paradox is that the "joke" was profoundly serious—deadly serious would perhaps be a more apt phrase—and what we call black humor today is the self-laceratingly painful response to a world that Jarry foresaw when he created 'Pataphysics. The laughter that stems from 'Pataphysics, like that brought about by contemporary black humor, is a barely opaque cover over the rictus of agony that is the true response to a world that makes no sense and that resists all attempts to impose sense on it since the marvelously ingenious concept of God has been vaporized. 'Pataphysics was not really developed until long after the full force of Jarry's prophetic vision had been made manifest, when the Collège de 'Pataphysique was founded in Paris in 1948. Jarry himself only gave it a name and a rudimentary definition before his early death.[22] According to Jarry, " 'Pataphysics is the science of imaginary solutions, which symbolically attributes the properties of objects, described by their virtuality to their lineaments."[23] A good deal of this is deliberate doubletalk, of course, but the salient point is that 'Pataphysics is the science of *imaginary* solutions. Not only are all the old solutions to the problems of the world (elsewhere in the same passage Jarry says that " 'Pataphysics is the science of the realm beyond metaphysics") inadequate or meaningless: no new ones can be found either. One must simply make up one's own. And these should not be looked on as binding either. Imaginary solutions, by definition, can exist simultaneously and change at will. Jarry once advised people faced with the task of filling out a form in quintuplicate to fill out each form separately with a different set of answers. This is not a rejection of the world and a retreat into the self, but a mocking, even wryly joyous, creation of alternate worlds. Man becomes the artist of life. In his imagination he recreates his surroundings to suit himself. Rather than attempt to define himself and then impose his conception of himself on the world (Strindberg and the expressionists) or fade the borders between his conception of reality and reality itself (Pirandello), he juggles chaos and molds it to his passing will.

An excellent example of this and of the replacement of metaphysics by 'Pataphysics is a short dialogue Jarry published in *Le canard sauvage* in which he concludes that the pope does not exist but is an invention of anticlerical journalists.[24] This is carried one step further in an elaborate mathematical proof that Jarry devised to demonstrate that the area of God is zero times the square root of zero. This leads to the definition of God as "the tangential point between zero and infinity."[25] The definition of what had been the symbol of omniscience and order as the tangential point between zero and infinity negated once and for all, and as starkly as possible, the possibility of hope and of faith in a salvation from the hideousness of man's visible fate. It was an attitude that would lead to the philosophical nihilism of Dada, to the desperate mockery of surrealism, or to the sardonic despair of absurdism. Jarry proclaimed a state of cosmic anarchy in which man floated aimlessly from birth to death, in which he himself and all he accomplished with his infantile social strivings ended only in the shower of artefacts and body parts that Artaud had shown in his symbolic vision at the beginning of his play *Le jet de sang*. God had had his head lopped off by the French Revolution which, by denying the divine right of kings, effectively ended the function of religion as a guiding force in public life. And the continued worship of his headless hulk with desperate and often hysterical adherence to ritualistic forms by the mass of the population, egged on by professionally interested acolytes of varying degrees of sincerity, was of scant significance for the thinker. The comforting assurance that had pervaded and permeated life for so many centuries had been blown away; the artificial lambency that had lighted man along his wished-for path had been replaced by vacuous night. Each man had now to create his own lamp and use its light to build his own path through the void.

Antonin Artaud's theater of cruelty is the outgrowth of the Jarryesque view of life. It is an attempt to come to terms with man's place in a void. Artaud sought to do this by exalting the universal self. It should be noted that this was not a solution of the problem that mankind now faced, for there is no solution to the unbearable (true tragedy, Ionesco noted, can be found only in the unbearable),[26] but simply a coming to terms. Where Strindberg and the expressionists sought refuge in the individual self and Pirandello asserted the primacy of each person's conception of his self and his view of reality, Artaud exalted the basic element that he believed existed at the core of every human being. As Artaud saw it, what was wrong with drama, as well as with all the other arts, was culture. By "culture" Artaud meant the overlay of artificialities that civilization had imposed upon human nature. The *essence* of human nature, its basic and intrinsic quality, had become obscured by the unreal formal masks—the socially acceptable behavior patterns arbitrarily imposed on us by custom and tradition. Since art is reality, the artist's task was to strip away the layers of artificiality and expose the core of reality that had been hidden for so long. To Artaud this core was pure emotion; and emotion was latent, instinctual savagery. He perceived that men are, as they always have been, basically barbaric, that the thick protective wall of urbane, civilized behavior they have acquired through centuries of hiding from psychological self-realization is easily crumbled by a forceful appeal to irrational emotion.

Culture, then, must be swept away. Only the instinctive human desires (anger, hate, longing, the physical desires, etc.)

are worthy of consideration by the artist. Everything must be elemental—culture and all it implies, including form in art, is out of harmony with instinctive human emotion. In Freudian terms Artaud looked on the ego and the superego as cultural artefacts; only the id was real and common to all humanity. The theater of cruelty was an attempt to seek the common denominator of mankind; after the stripping away of the layers of social behavior patterns comes the dissolution into the elemental howl: men becoming linked to each other through the recognition of their common animality. The function of theater was to protest against the artificial hierarchy of values imposed by culture by being consistently uninhibited and to demonstrate the true reality of the human soul and the relentless conditions under which it lives.

The manner in which this violent attack on the everyday is to be accomplished involves a fantastic, larger-than-life callousness that enables the characters to disregard the amenities of social behavior, and a rejection of speech as a means of communication. Speech, according to Artaud, is nontheatrical; therefore, strictly speaking, it has no place in the theater. What Artaud meant by this was that ever since the theater had descended (as he saw it) from ritual to art form, all the essentially theatrical elements—those elements that distinguish the theater from other forms of expression—had been subordinated to speech. Everything that has ever been done in the theater since ancient Greece has been predicated on the assumption that the function of the theater is communication through speech. But speech—communication of rational ideas—is the very thing that does not and cannot distinguish the theater from anything else—which makes it, in short, merely a branch of literature. If rational communication through speech is really the ultimate goal of the theater, then, according to Artaud, there is no point at all in going to the enormous trouble and expense of producing a play: it is obviously enough simply to read it. One can obtain information from the written word just as well as from the spoken. Theater, Artaud decreed, must be theatrical; and speech is not theatrical, but literary. Therefore we must concentrate exclusively on those elements of the theater peculiar to it alone.

To Artaud theater was something that had been perfect in its beginnings and had been degenerating ever since as a result of contamination by civilized conventions. Artaud felt that the theater had originally been the medium through which men expressed their unconscious feelings—the mysterious, nonrational essence of their beings. Like Jarry and like all the other avant-garde writers who came after him, Artaud looked at mankind in much the same way that Pascal did, although the latter drew radically different conclusions from his view: "*Condition de l'homme: inconstance, ennuy, inquiétude.*" The condition of man was such because of the unrelenting malignancy of the incomprehensible cosmic powers that govern him. Hence the theater, which must reflect the condition of man, must be a "theater of cruelty."

Cruelty in the theater does not mean, as Artaud was careful to emphasize, mere sadism: it is the impersonal, mindless— and therefore implacable—cruelty to which all men are subject. The universe with its violent natural forces was cruel in Artaud's eyes; and this cruelty, he felt, was the one single most important fact of which man must be aware. This cruelty is seen to some extent as viciousness between human beings. But such scenes must be presented in a manner calculated to purge the spectator of the corresponding emotions in him rather than to arouse in him the desire to imitate. At the same time, the spectator must be made aware of the violence dormant within himself and the omnipotence of the forces outside himself: each theatrical performance must shatter the foundations of the spectator's existence. It must show him his own helplessness in the presence of the awesome and ineluctable forces that control the world. The theater must entangle the emotions, for the majority of the people use their senses rather than their intellect. It must be *ecstatic*. It must crush and hypnotize the onlooker's senses. It must have the same effect on the audience as the dances of the whirling dervishes and the ritual incantations and ceremonies of black magic. Like these ceremonies, the theater must combine submission and mystic union with protest and defiance.

While there are obvious philosophical similarities in Dadaism, surrealism, and absurdism, they differ quite distinctly in their manner of treating the central problem that Jarry put into artistic terms and Artaud defined. Although Artaud decried the function of speech in the theater, he was a lucid expositor of his theories in writing and had by no means given up on language as a tool for communication entirely. The Dadaists, who developed independently of Artaud's theories, which did not become well known in artistic circles until after the Dada movement had effectively petered out, *did* give up on language entirely. Dada was started in Zürich in 1916 by a group of refugees from the war. These young men had come to neutral Switzerland from both sides in order to escape the horror and idiocy of a war they did not believe in and which they saw as having destroyed every remaining vestige of civilization. Diplomacy had corrupted language, and the slogans which were driving men to the battlefield had perverted it. They felt—and this was an attitude that outlived Dada and persists to this day—that language, both written and spoken, as a means for the transmission of ideas or for information on all but the most elementary functional level had become a dead issue. Those who still attempted to use it in the traditional manner and put their faith in its efficacy were tilting at windmills and falling into ditches. This view was encapsulated by the manner in which Tristan Tzara introduced Dada to Paris: standing on a stage, he read a newspaper to the audience while an electric bell kept ringing so that no one could hear what he was saying.[27] The negation of language by means of a modern mechanical artefact points its own moral here, although specific didacticism was never a purpose of the Dadaists. They wanted merely to shock—to do what Artaud was later to describe as breaking down the artificial social barriers in order to arrive at the inner core of the being.

Tzara was also making a specific reference here to the *type* of language to be found in newspapers: the language of slogans and mendacity that deserved to be drowned out by the bell.

The ultimate attack on language per se was made by Kurt Schwitters, a Dadaist to the core although never a member of the movement, and, with the fragmentational urge typical of the time, the founder of his own one-man "movement" which he called Merz. During a cabaret recital of his poems, Schwitters announced that he was going to recite his latest poetic work, held up a placard with the letter *W* painted on it, and proceeded to wail this letter in every conceivable tone.[28] There is an unconfirmed sequel to the story to the effect that he then turned the placard upside down and proceeded to hum the letter *M*. Amusing though the incident is, it is the ultimate expression of despair about the possibility of communication between human beings. Carl Laszlo, a contemporary post-Dadaist who, like Schwitters, founded his own movement, Panderma, achieved the paradox of poetically expressing this disintegration of language in his play *Essen Wir Haare* (Let's Eat Hair!): "The moon tenderly strokes the clouds. / The eagle flies low, with the night in its claws. / Dim, faraway stars are exploding. / A comet screams, 'Good-bye!' / The day has celebrated a marriage. / Death has kissed a maiden. / Language is tranquilly disintegrating . . . / The syllables . . . / We're disappearing . . . / Into the soft waves of the alphabet sea . . ."[29]

The negation of language is the most powerfully destructive symbolic negation of life possible. The man who does not believe in the instrumental efficacy of language believes in nothing. Gibberish and dumbness are the ultimate expressions of nihilism. Linguistic nihilism is matched by anatomical nihilism, a somewhat weaker expression of the philosophy except when transformed into such a superb multiple symbol as that occurring near the beginning of Artaud's *Le jet de sang*. Tzara uses this method in a slightly lighter vein in *Le coeur à gaz* (The Gas Heart). This play, which dates from 1920, has six characters: Eye, Mouth, Nose, Ear, Neck, and Eyebrow. Tzara's opening stage direction specifies that the play "will satisfy only industrialized imbeciles who believe in the existence of men of genius."[30] The dialogue is a deliberate farrago of nonsense, and plot there is none. The point is fragmentation: symbolically speaking, human beings do not exist anymore. They are divided into anatomical parts without reasoning powers, chattering aimlessly and nonsequentially.

Obviously, and indeed explicitly, a movement such as Dada is self-destructive. There have been sporadic attempts to revive Dada as an art form, principally by Richard Huelsenbeck, one of the movement's original founders and the leader of its subsequent activities in Berlin in the years immediately after the end of the war. Such attempts, however, contradict the very essence of Dada, which was an immediate and instinctive "gut" response to the shock of the First World War. That response was a total nihilistic rejection of society and of the art that is its expression. It substituted no plan for a new society and, consequently, no new art forms to express the spirit of such a society. It excoriated what existed to the ultimate degree of fragmenting not only the singularity of the body, but the individual spirit that inhabits it and the language by which it communicates; and, logically, it had to fragment itself. The conditions that inspired it have been duplicated a hundredfold in the years since it sprang up, but the shock value on which it depended for its effect has dissipated. Dadaism reborn can only repeat, but the spectacle of a house of cards destroyed by a cannonball decreases in effect in direct proportion to the number of shots.

The spirit that had moved Strindberg, the expressionists, Jarry, and the Dadaists, and was even then moving Artaud and Pirandello, was to manifest itself next in surrealism. It was a spirit of helpless groping in a void lashed by the mindless fury that had crumbled and scattered the illusion of the benign God. Strindberg and the expressionists had retreated into the self, the Dadaists had tried symbolically to destroy the existing order of the world, Pirandello was to seek reality in the theatrical artefact. The surrealists attempted to create a parallel world in which they would feel more at ease. Jarry was the precursor both of the destructiveness of the Dadaists and the pseudoplayful perverse creativity of the surrealists.

Surrealism, as the word indicates (it was coined by Apollinaire before his death in 1918), is the imposition of a "higher reality" on reality. The motivation is the same as in the other dramatic attitudes already discussed. Looking back on the beginnings of the movement of which he was the leading light, André Breton wrote in 1934, "Above all, we were blindly at the mercy of a systematic, embittered rejection of the condition under which we were compelled to live at that time. But this rejection did not stop there: it was greedy and knew no bounds."[31] The attitude is familiar: rejection of what *is* because of a disillusionment with the explanations that purported to justify it and give it meaning. The method adopted by the surrealists was different, however.

Surrealism was created by refugees from the foundering ship of Dadaism. The prior movement had been an instinctive reaction to the battle; Surrealism was a more contemplative reaction to the smoldering battlefield. Instead of attacking the world or trying to build it up again in a better way, the surrealists, as Breton says, chose to ignore it. Since one cannot live in a vacuum, however, one must construct one's own "reality" if the existing one is not satisfactory. That is what the surrealists did, and, luckily, the materials for the construction were just then at hand. The chief intellectual influences on surrealism were Henri Bergson's antirationalism and his theory of a mystical and indefinable "élan vital" as the motivating force in the human being; Einstein's theory of relativity, which neatly removed the plinth from the column of Newtonian physics and left it levitating as if in contradiction of its own theory of gravity; and Freud's theory of dreams, which convinced the surrealists that their task was to bring out the greater reality that lurked hidden away in the depths of the psyche.[32] As Breton put it retrospectively, "Surrealism brought forth new states of consciousness, . . . it . . . modified human feeling; it took a decisive step toward the unification of the personality, of that personality which was in the process of becoming more and more profoundly dissociated."[33] Freud's revelations about the dream as the area in which man reveals himself and the waking life as the area of repression exercised the deepest influence on the surrealists. The problem was not only to discover what the inner and higher reality consisted of but also to discover ways of bringing it out. The surrealists' solution to this problem was what they called "automatic writing." The point of this was to write whatever poured forth instinctively from the inner mind without the mediation of reason. Traditional reason was looked upon as the supreme corrupting influence by the surrealists. Frequently they eased the transition from the inner mind to the light of day with drugs, and many surrealist works were in fact written during drug-induced stupors. Such works constitute occasionally amusing contributions to the tradition of pure nonsense literature. As such, logically, they cannot be commented on; or, in the context of surrealist "logic," only by a critic who is himself in a drug-induced stupor. "Automatic" criticism is, however, fortunately a contradiction in terms since the critic, by the very nature of his profession, is, unlike the creative artist, condemned to live in the objective world and to interpret even illogicality in terms of the objective world's logic.

"Existence is elsewhere," Breton tells us, and the phrase might serve as a succinct summing-up of the essence of the surrealist philosophy. "Existence is elsewhere": it is in the reflection in the mirror; it is in the depths of the mind; it is in the antimatter in which every particle of the objective world has its counterpart. To find—or, rather, to create—that world of antimatter is the task of the surrealist. The surrealists, deriving their method from Jarry, practiced fragmentation by splitting. As with 'Pataphysics, on one side stood the material world, rejected; on the other, the antimatter world, created. "At certain times I have dreamed of an eraser with which to rub out the filth of humanity," wrote Louis Aragon in 1924.[34] In order to do this they turned their backs on the world and became completely self-absorbed. One biographer of Breton comments on the difficulty of arriving at any solid facts about the personal lives of the surrealists. Their own personal histories are without significance for them. Where they were and what they were doing in the world at any particular time are not important: only their state of mind at any particular time has any substantive meaning for them.[35] This sounds very much like the retreat into the mind that Strindberg, the expressionists, and Pirandello practiced, but there is a qualitative difference. The retreat of the others was motivated by an obsessive concern with the supreme importance of the writer's self, or with a desire to reshape the outside world in accordance with the writer's vision, or with the fragmentation of reality into a theoretically infinite number of personal visions. The retreat of the surrealists was motivated by a desire to create a counterworld within their minds. In its earliest and purest form surrealism was based on random thought associations, and its purpose was to show that the higher reality was based on chance—that there was no "meaningful" basis to human existence. Surrealism was seen as "an act of faith in the superior reality of certain forms of mental association and of the dream, both understood as totally free of any of the constraints that logic, ethics, or esthetic judgment usually impose."[36] Or, as Breton put it, "Pure psychic automatism by means of which it is hoped to express . . . the real functioning of thought. Dictation of thought, in the absence of any control exerted by reason, outside of all esthetic and moral preoccupation."[37] There was as yet no attempt to change man for the better, none of the hortatory spirit that crept into surrealism later when its leaders, Breton and Aragon, turned to Communism.

In a declaration dated January 27, 1925, and signed by twenty-six surrealists, including Breton, Aragon, Artaud, Desnos, and Peret, article 5 specified, "We have no intention of trying to change the way men act; we intend merely to show them the fragility of their thought, on what precarious bases, over what abysses, they have built their trembling houses."[38] For many of the declaration's signers this impersonal, disinterested attitude soon changed as they followed their infallible pope, Breton, into the Communist party. Breton's genius for public relations, his continuous advertisement of himself as the one and only leader and official spokesman of the surrealist movement, which he regarded as his personal property, has blinded literary historians to the fact that Breton was himself a surrealist for only a very short time. Belief in a political system, communication of concrete ideas through language, and revolution in the social sense are completely incompatible with the philosophy of surrealism as it originally was. The sobriquet of

"Pope" with which someone dubbed Breton is well advised, for he organized the movement and set rules for it (as early as 1925 there was a Bureau des Recherches Surréalistes at 15 rue de Grenelle, open every day except Sunday—interestingly—from 2:30 to 4:30),[39] admitting members and excommunicating them with the bland assumption of infallibility that characterized his Catholic counterpart. Under Breton, indeed, the history of the surrealist movement is very similar to that of the church: the movement that he founded had about as much substantive similarity to the movement that he ended up with as catacombal Christianity had to the Christianity of the Renaissance popes.

René Daumal, far more than Breton, was the archetypal surrealist. Daumal, who died in 1944 at the age of thirty-six, came to the surrealist movement when it was already well under way, but he believed the surrealist vision and wrote what he saw. Like most of the other surrealists, he experimented with drug-induced automatic writing, but his best work shows a disciplined mind creating an antiworld on the other side of the mirror.

Daumal's first book of poems had the surrealistically significant title *Contre-Ciel* (Counter-Heaven). With a little stretching it could also mean "Against Heaven." Both versions express the core of the surrealist spirit: implicitly destructive yet creative. What *is* must be rejected, yet what is created depends on it; surrealism attempts the concretization of the antiworld that is latent in this world and represents the mystical perfection that is immanent in it. The most perfect example of surrealist writing is Daumal's unfinished novel *Mont Analogue*, subtitled "A Novel of Symbolically Authentic Non-Euclidean Adventures in Mountain Climbing." We possess perhaps a quarter or a fifth of the novel Daumal intended to write, but it is enough to show that *Mont Analogue* would have been one of the most significant novels of the twentieth century.

The two chief characters of the book are the narrator (Daumal himself) and the symbolically named Pierre Sogol (*logos* spelled backward). The latter now earns his living by teaching mountain climbing—the ever-upward striving toward the mystical surreal ideal—though he was formerly a monk attached to a rather peculiar sect. The monastery was Sogol's first attempt to cleanse his mind of mundane dross; but the monastic way of separating the mind from the world is, as we learn toward the end of the fragment, precisely the wrong way to do it. There can be no salvation in loss of self; the self, or the sense of its existence, is all the human being possesses, and to cast it aside is to opt for nullity. Life in the monastery consists in the monks' attempt to avoid the wiles of the Tempter secretly appointed by the Father Superior. One day Sogol unwittingly falls victim to the Tempter when his inventive abilities are appealed to: "If only scientists today, instead of constantly inventing new means to make life easier, would devote their resourcefulness to producing instruments for rousing man out of his torpor!"[40] As a result of succumbing to the temptation of arousing man from his torpor, Sogol invents "a pen for facile writers which spattered or blotted every five or ten minutes; a tiny portable phonograph, equipped with an earpiece like those on hearing aids, and which would cry out at the most unexpected moments, 'Who do you think you are?'; a pneumatic cushion that I called 'the soft pillow of doubt,' and which deflated unexpectedly under the sleeper's head; a mirror whose curvature was designed . . . so as to reflect any human face like a pig's head."[41]

Sogol is finally expelled from the order because of his *"incurable need to understand."* [42] He has now decided that understanding is not enough, and he and the narrator have postulated the *necessary* existence of a mountain higher than any ever known on earth yet existing on earth and accessible to human beings. This mountain is the gateway to the (sur)real world that is greater than the real world and contains it. To reach the pure consciousness to be found on the slopes of Mount Analogue, in other words, is as a breakthrough from the contained to the container, from that which is immanent to that which subsumes it. Knowledge and understanding are separate from the mystical apprehension of the self, which must be kept discrete and inviolable. Sogol lives in a huge attic which is a carefully constructed compendium of human knowledge. Along the paths that wind through the attic knowledge is hung from cards as carcasses are hung from butchers' hooks:

> A diagram of a plant cell, Mendeleieff's periodic table of the elements, a key to Chinese writing, a cross-section of the human heart, Lorentz's transformation formulae, each planet and its characteristics, fossil remains of the horse species in series, Mayan hieroglyphics, economic and demographic statistics, musical phrases, samples of the principal plant and animal families, crystal specimens, the ground plan of the Great Pyramid, brain diagrams, logistic equations, phonetic charts of the sounds employed in all languages, maps, genealogies—everything in short which would fill the brain of a twentieth-century Pico della Mirandola. . . . Here, all this material was visibly outside of us; *we could not confuse it with ourselves.*[43]

Knowledge is outside; reality is inside. Science has failed, and all that is left is withdrawal into the self, into the world inside that is an analogue of the world outside, there to build an antiworld stripped of the dross that festoons reality like a shroud.

Sogol, the narrator, and some friends organize an expedition and finally find Mount Analogue (an elaborate "scientific" explanation on 'Pataphysical lines is given for its usual invisibility and its failure to show up on positional calculations). When they sail into the bay of Analogue Island, they discover that they have been watched from inside and judged worthy to enter. The island is inhabited by other people who have had the idea of climbing to seek the eternal truth and have reasoned that there must be a counterworld where it exists— and by their descendants, for there is no turning back to the world outside. Analogue Island has its generations and its history, going back to earliest human times, for there have always been people who have been dissatisfied with what is and have become convinced that there must be an Otherwhere that is pure and of which this world is only a dim reflection. The island is ruled by the Mountain Guides, who live high up, while the lower slopes and seacoast are inhabited by those who have failed in the attempt to climb or by their descendants, many of whom have never tried. The members of the expedition immediately become seduced by the temptation of knowledge, studying the peculiar flora and fauna of the island and the curious languages spoken there. The only object of any intrinsic worth on the island, the possession of which confers rank, is the peradam, a curved crystal stone that is usually found only on the highest slopes and is visible only to those that are worthy—i.e., to those who have approached the realization of self. This is illustrated when Sogol achieves the unprecedented feat of finding a peradam on the seashore at the very moment that he is voluntarily divesting himself of his authority as leader of the group and appealing for their help in order "to become what he is, without imitating anyone."[44] This is perhaps the key sentence in what we possess of the book and the key statement of the meaning of surrealism. It is the withdrawal into the self in order to find its unique reality by casting off the straitjacket of socially emblematic behavior.

Fragmentational drama follows two ancestral lines. Its progenitors are Strindberg and Jarry. Their aims are the same: rejection of a world that has become incomprehensible by fragmenting it and withdrawing into the self. Or, in other words, the substitution of the self for the cohesive principle that formerly held the bits and pieces of the world together in a satisfactory semblance of a coherent whole. The methods by which this is accomplished differ, however. Strindberg influenced the expressionists and Pirandello, for whom the mind is a subjective entity by means of which one can cope with the world. Jarry, through his invention of the "science" of 'Pataphysics, built up an objective world to replace the outside world, which he rejected no less fiercely than Strindberg and his followers. Dadaism took from him only the fierce rejection, and, offering no substitute of its own for what it destroyed, petered out and faded away. Surrealism followed Jarry's method more directly. Like Jarry, the surrealists built up an imaginary world of their own (" 'Pataphysics is the science of imaginary solutions") and turned their backs on the outside world to seek the "greater reality" of the self. The only difference was that with the surrealists there was an implied mystical faith in the possibility of attaining something better if only one succeeded in delving deep enough into the self.

During the 1930s and the subsequent war years, the sense of fragmentation was temporarily dormant. The delusive coherence given the order of the world first by dialectical materialism and then by the patriotic fervor engendered by the war was reflected in the drama of that time. But dialectical materialism was merely another form of religion, a crisis cult aroused by the Depression, with the Second Coming replaced by a Kingdom of the Proletariat, who were to emerge like troglodytes from the catacombs of the sweatshops to labor joyfully at the communal assembly lines and frolic in the rufous lambency of a classless future. As for the war dramas, like all war dramas, they were merely miracle plays brought up to date with the haloes replaced by helmets, the rack, stake, and thumbscrew by blood, sweat, and tears; and the celestial apotheosis by posthumous medals pinned on misty-eyed widows' breasts.

The aftereffect of the Second World War, however, was as devastating on the trend of intellectual thought as the actual experience of the first had been. The realization that the atrocities which the war had ended were not endemic in the ethos of a particular nation but had merely been brought by it to the highest pitch of modern mechanized efficiency, and the realization that the cost of victory was the invention of the ultimate weapon that could lead to total human extinction at the whim of the possessor, brought about the philosophy of despair, which had begun to be elaborated prophetically during the war years by Albert Camus.

It is now over forty years since Albert Camus crystallized philosophy with his *The Myth of Sisyphus*. Camus' contribution to philosophy could be compared to Hercules' activities in the Augean stables. His method was simpler, however. Whereas Hercules labored as mightily to restore the stables to their pristine cleanliness as philosophers have labored to solve the problems of existence, Camus disposed of them by merely pointing out something that no one had noticed before: that they were simply not there. The philosophical stables down through the ages were mirror images of the problems befuddling the minds of thinkers: fantastic cobwebby structures through which only the faintest rays of light intermittently gleamed. Subjects such as the first cause, the unmoved mover, the essence of matter, the sound made by one hand clapping, and similar abstract conundrums absorbed the minds of philosophical thinkers. All this had turned philosophy into a sort of three-dimensional chess game with the kings missing and the players desperately designing intricate checkmate combinations that invariably foundered on the absence of the object to be checkmated. Christopher Caudwell, who, had he lived, may well have surpassed Camus to become the finest mind of the twentieth century,[45] explained this by pointing out that the perception of reality has never been objective but has instead always been conditioned by the philosophy brought to bear on reality. In other words, one observes reality through lenses that have already been molded by the values of one's upbringing. A man's views can "only be realized through the categories of society and thus emerge with the grain of the epoch, however carved. . . . The theory of a man is his world-view, and ultimately informs and guides his every action—is, in fact, inseparable from it. It may not, however, be realized consciously as a world-view. Any new theory . . . because it is an extension of his world-view, necessarily is arranged within its categories, even if the arrangement bring about some transformation of them."[46] Caudwell's point, and it is well taken, is that all human discoveries (he was talking about physics in the quoted passage) are socially determined. At any particular time and place throughout human history only certain discoveries were possible. All breakthroughs in science and philosophy have been of a magnitude and direction that were predetermined by the socioeconomic conditions within which the thinker had been bred. It is, as Caudwell put it, impossible to have a theory without a philosophy; and the philosophy will then be implied in the theory.[47] All human progress has been of a crablike nature because of this reciprocal action of theory and philosophy: the theory straining to leap forward, the philosophy acting as a brake. In other words, all thought has been built up on a basis of given, a priori principles.

Camus was the first philosophical thinker to free himself of a priori principles. While it is to his credit that he did this, he could not have done it had he not lived at a time when this was possible. Camus was the heir—as all of us are now—of the breakdown in received values that began with the heliocentric theory and, after more than two centuries of steady erosion and frantic philosophical shoring up, culminated in the thunderous crash of the French Revolution. After the French Revolution's separation of church and state all religiously based thought was unconsciously motivated by a wistful nostalgia for the security of a universal meaning. After the demonstration of total war afforded by the 1914–1918 conflict even secular ethical systems based on an appeal to convenience became visionary. Religion, which had been the conscious or unconscious basis of all previous philosophical systems, became a formalized ritual to which some thinkers continued to cling with the desperation of shipwrecked survivors grasping a sodden spar in a merciless and shark-infested sea.

It was at this moment that Camus came along and swept the pieces off the board. The horrors of recent history had enabled the thinker who had the courage to do so to think without externally imposed a priori principles. In a world stripped of the metaphysical dimension there was only the human factor, only the consciousness of an apparently meaningless existence; and the pieces could now be arranged on the board anew without regard to rules. There were no rules. Hence Camus' epoch-making statement: "There is only one really serious philosophical problem: suicide. Deciding whether life is or is not worth living is to answer the fundamental question of philosophy. All the rest—whether the world has three dimensions or not, whether the mind can be divided into nine or twelve categories—comes later. These are games . . ."[48] All the rest . . . are games—only the value of life itself is important. *"Le reste . . . ce sont des jeux."*

Camus' demonstration of the necessity of life in *The Myth of*

Sisyphus is elegant, though some might say unnecessary. And there *is* that concern with whether life is or is not *worth* living, which seems to have the moral imperative of sunnier days skulking somewhere in the shadows behind it. That life has meaning and is worth living under whatever circumstances is the subject of Camus' argument, but it is also self-evident. Life has meaning because it is the only given quantity in our consciousness, albeit a morally neutral one. Life is itself and needs no other definition or any other significance than our consciousness of the physical qualities which it comprises. It needs no externally imposed meaning or justification, since it justifies itself and its meaning is contained in its attributes—is, therefore, coexistent and identical with it. The problem is how to return to that meaning and that consciousness of itself of which it has been robbed by the imposition of external justifications that have served no other purpose than to suppress the consciousness of life in the human being and substitute other values for it.

Nothing that is not freely willed can have a meaning rooted in itself. The philosophical argument about free will and determinism has always been conducted on an ethereal metaphysical level with speculations concerning man's relationship to God and whether God has granted man free will or whether God has predetermined man's actions and man's fate. These speculations now seem as quaint as Ptolemy's on the physical structure of the universe, all the more so because Ptolemy and the philosophical thinkers—the free-will advocates and the determinism advocates, the realists and the nominalists, indeed the whole host of philosophical projectors and speculators—were dropped from the same mold. A belief in God and in God-given absolute values of one sort or another was impressed into them as if with a die upon putty so that their elaborate proofs are really desperate demonstrations that what they had been taught from childhood on was indeed true. Any other course would have been both physically dangerous and psychologically intolerable. *"Commencer à penser, c'est commencer d'être miné,"* Camus has said.[49] If this is true—and it seems to me not only true but a psychological truism—then all past philo-

sophical thinking has been a frantic, if frequently subconscious, fight to avoid thought. It has been instead a struggle to
justify and affirm; but thought by its very nature is destructive.
Thought is the contemplation and analysis of the thing-in-
itself. To think is to have the courage to discard preconcep-
tions and to risk being undermined by the result. Not the fear
of the Lord but the rejection of all metaphysical dross is the
beginning of wisdom. To think as all philosophers of the past
have thought is like examining a patient without undressing
him.

With the reflection in dramatic form of Camus' philosophy
the staging theories of Antonin Artaud finally came into their
own. During the heyday of his literary and critical activity in
the 1920s, Antonin Artaud had played the role of a prophet. It
is the nature of prophets to be ahead of their times; and as a
consequence their contemporaries tend to look upon them as a
bit loony. Artaud helped that impression along by displaying
some indisputably genuine aberrant behavior, although the
paranoia from which he suffered may well have been justifiably fortified to some extent by the delicately turned cold
shoulders to which he was often enough subjected. Artaud had
come up through the ranks of the avant-garde movements of
his day—he had been associated particularly closely with surrealism—and had been dragooned out of them when their
shallowness failed to satisfy his expectations. For there is no
doubt that Artaud was a prophet and saw deeper into the
nature of things than the offhandedly nihilistic poseur Tzara
or than that shrewdly calculating organizer of mockery, Breton. Artaud saw into the abyss of absurdity long before Camus
explored it and mapped it out. Artaud did not shy away from
this vision: he accepted it and affirmed it. He made it his
mission to bring a perception of this vision to his fellow men by
theatrical means.

Camus' assertion that life does have meaning and is preferable to death is not necessarily the formula for the elixir of
happiness. To say that life means itself is to assert that its
meaning is contained in the physical and mental sensations
comprising it at any given moment. But the eschatological

dimension has been removed. Life no longer could mean anything beyond itself; no longer could it be a preparation for a better life to come. Man may be happy in the revelation of the immediate moment, but he cannot refer beyond that moment; and his happiness, such as it is, is bound to the indeterminate and unpredictable succession of his moments. "Men die; and they are not happy," Camus wrote in 1938 in his play *Caligula*. The happiness of the immediate moment is necessarily fleeting and delusionary; ultimately there can be no happiness in a world where each man is imprisoned in his own impenetrable monad subject to extinction without reason. This view of life could lead only to a condition of total catatonic stasis or return to an even more rigid, though godless, formulation than before. As we shall see when we consider synthetic drama, this is indeed happening. Desperation at the comfortlessness of freedom bred the inevitable reaction of self-enslavement to new eschatological constructs.

Artaud's method was the theater of cruelty, which essentially meant showing life as it is, stripped of all embellishments. It meant, in other words, showing that men die and are not happy, for that is all the certain knowledge that is left after the facilely comforting and spurious assumptions of religion and society have been swept away.

Man with the teleological dimension removed, without the hope of an eschatological apotheosis, is the theme of Samuel Beckett's works. Beckett has formed precise images—images that seem chiseled in ice and suspended in a crystalline and frozen void—that are concrete complements of Camus' vision of the agonized writhings of man in an alien setting. Man, Camus seems to be saying, is an accidental, cursed with mind, set down within a mindless and therefore intrinsically indifferent essential: the physical universe. Here he can never be at peace because he is driven to understand and explicate the incomprehensible and inexplicable. Deprived of the infantile myths his forefathers invented to numb themselves to the realization of the unbearable, stripped of the comforting anesthesia of the robotlike rituals that he mimed for millennia in celebration of those myths, he has found himself engulfed by reality and found it more arcane than his most ingenious mythic contrivances. He has found chaos incarnate.

Beckett has two principle ways of showing man in the setting of chaos: the sense of temporary suspension in timelessness and the fragmentation of the physical being. We must remember that for Beckett these are not mere imaginative philosophical metaphors, but symbolic encapsulations of reality. Vladimir and Estragon are the real essences of which we are the shadows. The tragedies of everyday life do not concern Beckett, are no part of the absurdist vision. All that has been left far behind for the absurdist thinker. Friedrich Dürrenmatt puts the absurdist's attitude to traditional tragedy with his usual sardonic humor in his "Dramaturgische Überlegungen" to the revised edition of his *Die Wiedertäufer* (The Anabaptists). Reflecting on how Beckett would have treated a traditional tragic theme such as the death of Captain Scott and his companions on their South Pole expedition, Dürrenmatt concludes that Beckett would have shown the tragedy as having already taken place: Scott and his companions would be encased in separate blocks of ice with Scott speaking into the void, receiving no answer and having no awareness of being heard.[50] Neither Vladimir and Estragon nor Hamm and Clov have quite reached this point, but by the time we get to Krapp and Winnie we are much closer to this state of total catatonic stasis, of suspension in the void. This state is the closest we can get to the ideal state of lifeless timelessness that precedes and follows life. In a world patently without meaning beyond the individual's physical sensations, where men stumble over and grind to finer dust beneath their heels the rubble that once was fused into the seemingly substantial structure of religion and morality, all that they can do is mark time and wait.

Beckett postulates a cosmic malignity that is not an embodied sadistic God but simply a convenient metaphoric explanation for the human condition. There is a well-known Anglo-Saxon poem that forms an instructive contrast to Beckett's view. The poet compares life to a warm, brightly lit hut and the life of man to a sparrow that flies out of the cold darkness through the hut and out the other side again. Christian orthodoxy might quibble with this, but the point is that the poet saw life as warm and pleasant. Beckett uses the same image of passing through life, but he does not see it as a warm, comforting place. For him the void before birth is clearly preferable to life, and the act of procreation is to be condemned for roiling the ineffable calm of the inconceivable preexistent void. As Molloy puts it in the novel of that name, "I know she did all she could not to have me, except of course the one thing, and if she never succeeded in getting me unstuck, it was that fate had earmarked me for less compassionate sewers." Or, as Hamm and Clov put it in *Endgame*, "Did you ever have an instant of happiness?" "Not to my knowledge." A little later Hamm says, "Use your head, can't you, use your head—you're on earth, there's no cure for that." There is no mystical longing here for an ideal state of extinction. Suicide would be easy enough as a solution—theoretically. As Hamm says, there is no cure for being on earth: we are trapped within our minds, which are programmed (accidentally? deterministically? does it matter?) to function along logical paths. And as Camus has demonstrated, suicide is not logical for it represents no choice. For suicide dementia is a prerequisite. Absurd man is trapped within life and can only play games while he waits for the unknowable to arrive.

Vladimir and Estragon play the game of waiting for an entity that they have invented to "save" them from the unknowable. They have even hired the boy/priest to reassure them at regular intervals that they are not waiting in vain. Meanwhile they eat, sleep (and have nightmares), engage in futile philosophical discussions, and otherwise parody human existence. In Beckett we have gone beyond the fragmentation of society and the preoccupation with personal death that can still be seen in Ionesco. In Beckett's plays the characters themselves are symbols of the disintegration of human beings brought to a realization at last of their nescience and nullity, their baffled helplessness in the grip of the inexorable malignancy eating away at the flesh that is their sole barrier against extinction. Beckett's symbolic depiction of human fragmentation is far more serious and mordant than the comparatively self-indulgent japeries of

Tzara's *Le coeur à gaz,* which is to Beckett's vision as a cartoon is to a fully realized painting. To call one's characters Eye, Mouth, Nose, Ear, Neck, and Eyebrow, as Tzara does, is to make a statement and leave it at that. Such a statement is as meaningful and effective when the play is described as when it is performed.

With Beckett, however, the existential malaise is part of the physical makeup of the characters. Hamm is not a Nose: he is blind and paralyzed. Nagg and Nell, once vigorous progenitors, are intermittently animated blobs of senile decrepitude appropriately housed in garbage cans. Clov cannot sit down and always feels vaguely unwell. Winnie is gradually buried deeper and deeper in the sand of the wasteland, while her inexhaustible good humor and her relentless enthusiasm for triviality become ever more poignant to an audience that is sobered by her demonstration of its own self-anesthetizing devices. Lucky is reduced to an animallike state in which signs of a former humanity can still be seen faintly gleaming. Pozzo, the false Godot, returns blind and helpless. The Unnamable is a limbless torso dangling in the breeze, ruminating on the senselessness of being. The three characters in *Play* are disembodied heads sticking out of funerary urns delivering mutually exclusive monologues, rather like the icebound characters in Dürrenmatt's sardonic commentary. The list could go on and on with the dying Malone, the amorphous Molloy, the dropsical Mrs. Rooney, and the twenty-eight crippled Lynches in *Watt,* but the point is clear enough. To be born is to be condemned to death. It is, as Molloy puts it, to be "earmarked for less compassionate sewers" than the cloaca that is the aborted foetus's destiny—a point emphasized by Murphy when he specifies that his ashes be flushed down the toilet of the Abbey Theater during a performance, the reality of the "burial" making an ironic contrast with the imitative shadow play of life going on outside. For Beckett the life of man within the bounds of time—implying, as it does, finiteness and therefore meaninglessness—is as much a shadow play as the theater is to finite, timebound man. The image that best illustrates all of Beckett's work, particularly his most recent, is that of an inward-turning spiral that must eventually reach the vanishing point—complete stasis. Eventually Beckett may well feel moved to produce a work called *Period* consisting of a dot in the lower-right-hand corner of a blank page. When that happens literature as a reflection of the world will have been negated; by implication the world will no longer exist. In other words, the ultimate logical endpoint of the fragmentational view of the world will have been reached. The nonexistence of an essence of life will be implied—although, of course, the world will continue to appear to exist as a series of accidentals without the basis of an ultimate meaning beyond themselves. Literature and philosophy will have become like the black holes of the astronomers: an all-encompassing point where nothing is reflected and everything is absorbed and deadened.

CHAPTER 2

Analysis

The analytic writers represent the antithesis to the thesis of the fragmentational writers. Neither would have been possible without the collapse of traditional thought brought about by the intellectual shock waves of the French Revolution. The writers who stemmed from the fragmentational mentality saw that the traditional basis of society lay in fragments, and, whether they celebrated it or lamented it, accepted the fact. With no map to consult any longer as to the ultimate configuration of reality and their place in it, they chose either to distort the previous one or to ignore it. Those who stemmed from the analytic mentality tried to discover what the configuration of reality *really* was and to draw an entirely new map. For them the ruins were a sign of hope, for this time the pieces could be put together properly, the useless ones could be discarded, and new ones could be molded to fill the gaps in the new structure. When Humpty-Dumpty fell, the fragmentational writers concluded that he had been levitating all this time on the imaginary wall of faith; the analytic writers came to the same conclusion, but they did not despair as a result. They determined to put him together again after all, and this time perch him on a new, solid wall of fact. It was not for nothing that G. K. Chesterton described George Bernard Shaw as a man wearing boots that were too tight for him trying to walk on eggshells without breaking them. The analytic writers were trying to walk among the brittle shards of history and fit them together again, this time on a basis of sensible, factual, pragmatic reality.

Just as Strindberg was the "father" of the twentieth-century fragmentational drama, so Henrik Ibsen was the "father" of the twentieth-century analytic drama. Strindberg shrank within himself to create his dramatic world; Ibsen reached out and tried to transform the world. The attitudes were diametrically opposed, yet they were both radical departures from the attitudes that had been possible in the theater before them. The irony that one uncovers in comparing them is the fact that, opposed though they are, neither attitude would have been possible earlier. Both are the results of the changes in philosophical *Weltanschauung* that had taken place gradually and subconsciously in thinking minds with the filtering out of the faith in ultimate suprahuman values that constituted the effects of the scientific and French revolutions. With Strindberg and his followers, as we have seen, this resulted in a rejection of the previous intellectual topography of the world. With Ibsen and his followers it resulted in the attempt to construct a new intellectual topography. The intellectual world was now as much virgin territory to be explored as the physical world was to the Renaissance seafarers.

As early as 1891 Henry James saw quite clearly what Ibsen was trying to do: "He has cleared up the air we breathe and set a copy to our renouncement; has made many things wonderfully plain and quite mapped out the prospect."[1] James was one of the few who understood what Ibsen was trying to do. Ibsen laid down no specific program: he tried to describe the new configuration of reality as he saw it. Shaw, in his brilliant and deliberately wrongheaded polemic, *The Quintessence of Ibsenism*, tried valiantly to twist Ibsen's meaning so as to make him a forerunner of what Shaw intended to become. But Shaw too ended up in generalizations, as we shall see. Shaw started with the street maps he tried to convince his readers that Ibsen had drawn, but he too ended up projecting cosmic charts.

The key to understanding Ibsen's work subsequent to *Emperor and Galilean, Brand,* and *Peer Gynt* is to realize that he was an early existentialist. Ibsen's attempt to describe the world and analyze what was wrong with it was always earth centered. What mattered—the only thing that mattered—as Ibsen saw it, was the manner in which the individual comported himself within the given conditions of life. Redemption and repentance had become a phantasm; only the life of the human being mattered any longer. Since he wrote tragedies, his theme was failure *in* life—and its causes. When Ibsen wrote, this was not yet a subject that was accepted as the *Stoff* of popular dramatic literature. The resistance he met with from reviewers and the accusations of immorality that were directed against him, particularly in the cases of *A Doll's House* and *Ghosts,* were due to his insistence on presenting his characters as morally responsible only to themselves for their actions.

In Ibsen's view the necessary prerequisite to a new intellectual topography that took into account the absolute finiteness of the human condition was human self-responsibility. The generally pessimistic tone of his plays is due to his realization that men were still mired in the habits of the past, unable to break away from social and intellectual conventions that had been erected in the context of a set of arbitrary a priori principles. His plays are object lessons in how not to attain self-realization in a life that means nothing but itself. They are portraits of insufficient men and women, characters whose deficiency is that they cannot find the way out of the labyrinth of the past. The task of the reader or spectator of Ibsen's plays is to formulate for himself the synthesis corresponding to the thesis of the character's given social circumstances and the antithesis of that character's reaction against them. Although the final decision is left to the reader or spectator, there are, of course, definite indications in the plays of Ibsen, Shaw, and Brecht, the leading playwrights of the analytic school, as to which way the decision should go. It is for this reason that Ibsen was so regularly accused of immorality. He was always seeking to substitute a new morality for the old one, an existentially-based one for the authority-based one. Outbursts such as Ibsen faced when *Ghosts* was first produced in England are explained by Shaw's definition of morality as relative and dynamic. "Whatever is contrary to established manners and customs is immoral. An immoral act or doctrine is not necessarily a sinful one: on the contrary, every advance in thought and conduct is by definition immoral until it has converted the majority. For this reason it is of the most enormous importance that immorality should be protected jealously against the attacks of those who have no standard except the standard of custom . . ."[2] The "immorality" that Ibsen produced consisted in the rejection of social formulas and the assertion that everyone must work out his own destiny in the world and go straight toward it.

Ibsen's first fully realized plays are *Brand, Peer Gynt,* and *Emperor and Galilean. Brand* appears to be a play about a man who moves inexorably toward the goal he has set for himself but loses his humanity and finally his life. He is the first of Ibsen's many carriers of the "banner of the ideal"—a more serious version of the fatuous Hilmar Tönnesen in *Pillars of Society.* Most commentators have seen *Brand* and *Peer Gynt* as thematic companion pieces. Brand the fanatical idealist and Peer Gynt the cynical opportunist are seen as representatives of the opposite ends of the characterological spectrum in this view. Ibsen was supposedly espousing a pragmatically based Golden Mean by showing the disastrous consequences of extreme conduct in the two protagonists. This theory, which, with slight modifications, is held by almost every critical commentator, profoundly underestimates the enigmatic quality of

Ibsen's thought. It is not Brand's fanaticism that Ibsen shows us disapprovingly. Brand's single-mindedness causes him to sacrifice his child, his wife, his mother's hope of salvation, his parishioners, and, finally, himself. It brings him to disaster, dehumanizes him, and destroys him literally in the end as he immolates himself in the symbolic ice avalanche. It is tempting to interpret Brand's tragedy as the result of his stubborn disregard of the emotional amenities of human intercourse and of his monstrous perversion of his priestly mission from service through charity to salvation through chastisement. But Ibsen's point was always the necessity for existential decision; and Brand makes no such decision. Everything he does is caused by the intensification of his original decision to subjugate himself to an external entity. Brand starts out as a minister of the Christian religion, becomes dissatisfied with what he conceives to be the halfhearted degree of subjugation required by that religion in its present decadent state, and sets out, not unlike the fanatically self-lacerating ascetics of the early church, to purify himself and those around him. He aspires to be a St. Simeon Stylites of the Glaciers. Brand acts in accordance with a code of conduct that exists independent of him and that he accepts uncritically. His mission is to strip that code of the worldly dross with which it has become encrusted and return it to its original purity. Ibsen gives Brand a character that leads him to live with an obsessive fanaticism in the service of religion, but the essential point is that Brand is no more his own man than the vacillating and unprincipled opportunist Peer Gynt is. The irony of *Brand* is that Ibsen put the message he was to preach all his life in his protagonist's mouth and then shows him to be corrupting it with his own actions. When Brand says, "There is but one law / For all men: No cowardly compromise!"; when he says, "A man must be himself"; and when he describes the Mayor, an early sketch of Peter Stockmann, as ". . . a typical man of the people; / Full-blooded, right-thinking, well-meaning, energetic, / Jovial and just. And yet, no landslide, flood, / Or hurricane, no famine, frost or plague / Does half the damage in a year that that man does. / How much spiritual aspiration / Has he not stifled at birth?" he defines the creed Ibsen was to preach. Brand himself betrays that creed with his actions, for he interprets it as a charge to enslave himself completely to a "Higher Power."[3] Like Peer Gynt, Brand lives out his own fantasy, which is that of making himself the hero-object of his own life. But basically Brand is a portrait of a nonman for the existential thinker Ibsen. None of his decisions are his own. His Christian fanaticism becomes so intense that it turns him against what he believes to be the degeneration of Christianity and leads him to create a personal religion that is little more than a desperate and unthinking hysteria. Ibsen's portrait of him was part of his lifelong struggle of writing himself painfully into his own truth. Brand and Peer Gynt are not opposites: they are two sides of the same coin. Both characters exemplify existential indecision, the ultimate sin in all of Ibsen's plays. *Peer Gynt* is the central play of Ibsen's work and of the analytic drama in general. As such, it is one of the two or three most influential plays of the modern theater.

The "modern" or twentieth-century drama has no one single starting point. It could be argued that it had its first aborted birth pangs back in the 1830s when Woyzeck informed the Captain that morality was a function of economics. The fragmentational drama indubitably had one of its beginnings in 1896 when Jarry's Ubu coined what might be called his *mot de Crambronne.* Another starting point, this time for the analytic drama, occurred in 1867 when Peer met the Boyg in the second act of *Peer Gynt* and, as a consequence of his reaction to that encounter, peeled his symbolic onion in the fifth.

The Boyg is easily Ibsen's most puzzling creation. Critics seem to be baffled by him almost without exception and usually end up doing the same fatal thing Peer does—going round about him and proceeding to more profitable pursuits. Typical of the reaction to this most mysterious and enigmatic of the products of Ibsen's imagination is F. L. Lucas'. The wording here is itself revealing of the extent of the critical inability to come to grips with the problem of the Boyg: "What exactly does the Boyg signify? . . . perhaps the Boyg may suggest the prevaricating circuitousness of characters like Peer. . . . Later, in Egypt, Peer, seeing the Sphinx, will identify it with the Boyg. Are both Boyg and Sphinx, then, the mystery of human perversity?—that weakness of man, which is often man's escapeless fate? . . . it seems meant to embody Peer's own evasiveness; but it suggests also human evasiveness in general."[4] Lucas offers here a sort of catchall interpretation. The Boyg is Peer's "prevaricating circuitousness." This is later reworded as Peer's evasiveness and broadened to encompass all human evasiveness. Meanwhile we are asked if the Boyg does not perhaps represent human perversity, which is somehow identified with the "weakness of man, which is often man's escapeless fate." Lucas is by no means alone in retreating into an account of his table talk with himself when baffled by the text. Georg Groddeck, giving a psychoanalytic interpretation, tells us that the Boyg is "the self, the objective self, the opposite to the ego; he cannot be destroyed. *Or can he? Who knows?*"[5] For a psychoanalytic critic Groddeck is unusually humble about his abilities, though he reverts to form immediately after the quoted passage by tossing off a suggestion that the Boyg is *both* a birth and death symbol because he is described at one point by Peer as "narrow": "Narrow is the path at birth, narrow the way to the grave."[6] There is really little one can do with the feverish imagination of psychoanalytic critics.

Brian Downs does little more than to say that the Boyg is a "Voice and a Presence," whereas James Hurt calls it "as powerful an image of engulfment as appears in Ibsen's work."[7] None of this is very helpful, though both Downs and Hurt suggest that the whole Boyg scene should be played as a dream since it represents a conflict within Peer's mind. I do not myself think it matters particularly whether this scene and the previous one in the Troll King's court is played as a dream or not. What is certain is that both scenes are central to the development of the drama since they objectify the conflict in Peer's mind, and the decisions he makes in these scenes determine the future course of his life—and, by the same token, the moral that Ibsen wished to convey.

Neither the Boyg scene nor the one immediately preceding it in the Troll King's court has been adequately understood and interpreted by non-Norwegian critics. One of the stumbling blocks to a proper understanding of the Boyg scene is the fact, generally passed over in critical commentaries, that the Boyg is also a troll. Trolls in Norwegian folklore are thoroughly evil, misshapen creatures with a distinctly satanic cast to their personalities. The feast in the Troll King's hall is by no means the miniaturized Valhalla parody it becomes in the descriptions of English critics, but a diabolic Pandemonium peopled by figures from the imagination of Hieronymus Bosch. These trolls are "supernatural beings, akin to the enemies of the gods in the heathen world . . . they look . . . like Polyphemuses and the Cyclops in the *Odyssey*—huge, clumsy, and ugly. . . . The trolls are dangerous and brutal . . . [and] may be said to represent the evil forces in Nature . . . embodying or symbolizing those powers of evil, hidden in the soul of Man, which may at times suddenly suppress his conscious will and dominate his actions."[8] At the Troll King's court Peer learns the first principle of trolldom: "Be sufficient unto yourself"—that is, develop only yourself for your own ends in opposition to the human (Ibsen's) motto, "Be thyself." To be oneself in this context is to develop one's own individuality with due regard to one's responsibilities as a member of a whole: the human race. The human version leads to a full development of personal potentiality in relation both to oneself and to others; the troll version leads to the obsessive rapacity of the power-seeking self-aggrandizer that Peer later personifies as an amoral business tycoon.

   The Boyg scene is even more important than the scene in the Troll King's court, both for the development of Peer's character in the play and for the development and crystallization of Ibsen's thought. The scene with the Boyg sets the philosophical tone for all the rest of Ibsen's work, and all his subsequent drama is arguably an elaborate working out of the principle enunciated in that scene. The Boyg is another troll (the word is derived from a root meaning "curved"),[9] one of those unearthly beings that Ibsen used at many places in his poetry as "symbols of those powers of evil which he constantly felt living around him *and in himself*."[10] Like any writer who aims for more than ephemeral popularity, whether his purpose is to justify the ways of God to man or to proclaim that whatever is, is right, or to reject objective reality and substitute a personal vision, or to analyze reality and amend it for the better, Ibsen wrote to exorcise his personal demons. In Peer Gynt's scene with the Boyg we see what those demons were: the cowardly tendency to succumb to imposed circumstances and reject the integrity of the self. Ibsen never succeeded in defeating those demons in his life but achieved a sublimated victory over them in his work.

After the trolls disappear and their hall crumbles when the sound of church bells is heard—a traditional poetic device that it is hard to believe that Ibsen used as anything but a convenience—Peer finds himself alone in utter darkness. He is heard "slashing and hitting about him with a branch of a tree,"[11] apparently struggling with some invisible barrier. Something viscous and all-encompassing stands in his way; an evil presence that envelops Peer and mocks him, repelling him with its amorphous and apparently impassable mass. Three times its voice identifies itself as "Myself," adding once, "Can you say as much?" before it announces that it is "The great Boyg." Twice it speaks the famous words, so sinister in the full context of Ibsen's meaning, "Go round about, Peer!" What does all this mean? Was Ibsen really using the troll figures from Norwegian folklore literally, or was he using them to externalize the conflicts in Peer's mind? The only sensible interpretation of this scene, as well as of the preceding one, is that it occurs in Peer's mind. The scene with the Boyg is in a sense a classical rite de passage for Peer, whom Ibsen intended as his version of Everyman. When the Boyg thrice says that he is "Myself" he means that he is the essence of Peer/Everyman, the central id, the core of inertia in the human being that, if yielded to, winds down to the utter entropy that Peer later finds when he peels the onion. For the tragedy of Peer/Everyman is that he does yield to the Boyg. It is easier to "go round about," to slide around obstacles, to seek excuses for the failure to confront, to shirk the self-rending task of mobilizing the inertia at the root of the matter of which one is composed than to manufacture one's own unique identity. When the Boyg adds, "Can you say as much?" to his identification of himself as "Myself" it is the id speaking to the superego. Peer/Everyman's superego is not strong enough, and he succumbs and goes round about, as do the protagonists of so many other Ibsen plays. Although Peer rejects the Troll King's offer in the previous scene and will not permit his eyes to be slit so that he can see reality from the troll point of view, ironically he merges with the Boyg, another troll, and lives out his life going round about in order to be sufficient unto himself alone. Thus Peer/Everyman commits the greatest sin of all: he betrays the possibility of the development of the human integrity that lies within him; and thus when, in the last act at the end of his misspent life, he peels the onion, he finds the same void at the core as there is within him, for he has lived all his life with the amorphous evasiveness, molding himself to external needs, that the Boyg represents. And so his fate is to be melted down in the ladle of the implacable Button-Molder and be as if he had never been.

Ibsen's very first critics sensed his intention unconsciously, and it is that feeling of theirs rather than their loudly proclaimed outrage at the supposed destruction of familial values in *A Doll's House* and *Ghosts* that accounts for the viciousness and unbridled intemperance of their denunciations. Though they did not analyze it in those terms, what alarmed them was that Nora walking out on her family was not going round about, was being herself and not just enough of herself to get by. It was the replacement in individual psychological terms of a tried, trusted, and *safe* old order by a new one that might lead anywhere. What had been cohesive and whole, an accepted mode of belief encompassing all aspects of life, was being analyzed, broken down into its component parts in the hope that something better could be built with them.

Ibsen's analytic bent showed itself in dramatic terms in the psychological characterization of his protagonists. Brian Downs has pointed out that Ibsen's attitude to Peer is sardonic and impassive in contrast to the usual attitude of authors to epic heroes.[12] This attitude is typical of the analytic writer: Peer Gynt is not a "hero" but a subject to be dissected in order to show where and how he has failed to be "heroic." In Peer's case, as I have tried to show, that failure lies in his inability to make a personal existential decision with respect to his path in life, symbolized by his subjugation to the Boyg. Ibsen's tendency was to model his protagonists on Peer. The thread of tragedy that binds his plots is due to the failure of his characters in their struggle for self-emancipation. In each of his plays the Boyg looms, an invisible, and intangible suffocating presence. Only in *A Doll's House* and *An Enemy of the People* is he overcome, although in *Ghosts* the corrosive folly of submitting to him is acknowledged.

A Doll's House is as straightforward a play as Ibsen ever wrote. Nora is the true Ibsenian heroine, for she grows from an unthinking epigone of all that is conventionally accepted, a human doll that automatically goes "round about," into a human being capable of selecting her own alternatives, a personification of existential force. Her slamming of the door has often been called symbolic; and that it is, for practical it certainly is not. It is her rite de passage from infantile helplessness to maturity and responsibility. The basic existential position that is instinctively latent in Ibsen's thought is that existence precedes essence. This has become almost an intellectual truism now, but in Ibsen's day the idea embodied in that truism, though it was not expressed in those terms, was revolutionary. Nora's psychological transition consists in a realization for the first time in her life that she *exists* and that that fact is the primary one that she must consider. Like most people, she had never consciously realized this obvious and elementary fact and had lived—as her husband continues to do—as a bundle of imposed false essences. Michael Meyer, writing of this play as well as of *Ghosts* and *An Enemy of the People*, puts it simply and clearly: "their true theme [is] . . . the need of every individual to discover the kind of person he or she really is, and to become that person."[13] The only quibble one might have with this statement is that it should not be applied only to the three plays in question: it applies equally to all the works of Ibsen's maturity, although in the other plays he concentrated on dealing with the consequences of the failure to become oneself. The question of what Nora does after slamming the door, presumably plowing through the midnight snowdrifts with no place to go, has preoccupied many critics with incurably realistic minds. But Nora does not go out into the snow with no money and no prospects: the actress playing Nora goes offstage, and the character she plays becomes another character whom we must imagine. Not a wintry night but another psychological plane of reality lies on the other side of that famous door; and what Ibsen's character does there is "think out, in independence and solitude, her position in a world whose general laws she has begun to apprehend and means to fathom."[14]

Dr. Stockmann in *An Enemy of the People* is already halfway round the corner that Nora turns when his play begins. The Boyg, Nora discovers, disappears—vaporizes—when one walks boldly up to it and through it instead of going round about. Dr. Stockmann has never gone round about. He has never been conscious of the Boyg in his mind. He starts out as a bullheaded, vain, tactless, amiable, and well-meaning fellow acting instinctively and impulsively—a perfect foil for his stuffy and utterly conventional brother. "You have an ingrained tendency to take your own way," his brother, the mayor, complains, ". . . and that is . . . inadmissible in a well-ordered community. The individual ought . . . to acquiesce in subordinating himself to the community—or, to speak more accurately, to the authorities who have the care of the community's welfare."[15] Peter Stockmann represents the ultimate in the nonexistential view of life: he is a personification of the Boyg. The comic aspects of Dr. Stockmann's personality, dramatically effective on the stage, have led critics in many instances to judge the play as nonserious and even to interpret it as a satire on the single-minded idealist, with Dr. Stockmann as a farcical version of Gregers Werle in *The Wild Duck*. This is, I believe, a serious mistake. *An Enemy of the People* is Ibsen's most profoundly felt and directly meaningful play. Dr. Stockmann's speech in the fourth act, in which he excoriates the majority and exalts the intellectual minority, represents his own psychological transition from instinctive man to existential man. Before, he follows his impulses; now he analyzes and makes decisions. That he has not acquired either diplomacy or shrewdness in the process is irrelevant: he has acquired himself. Practically speaking, he will probably fail; personally, he has triumphed, for, like Nora, he has found himself and will now *make* himself. When he says at the end that "the strongest man in the world is he who stands most alone," there is not a hint of irony in the words: he is uttering Ibsen's own most deeply felt creed. The irony comes in much earlier, in act 2, when Hovstad, the hypocritical newspaper editor, says, "There is one thing that I esteem higher than [good intentions] and that is for a man to be self-reliant and sure of himself." That, of course, is the one thing that the newspaper editor is not. Dr. Stockmann is, and in the course of the play he becomes conscious of himself as well.

The protagonists of most of Ibsen's other late plays all show the failure of existential self-realization and of the resultant self-emancipation. It is Ibsen's portrayal of the negation of his ideal that has given him his stature as a tragic artist. Ibsen's point, the essence of his pioneering modernism in the theater, that the human being must stand alone since there is no support other than his own self-created integrity, is exemplified in the necessity of rejecting what we might call "boygness"—the tendency to go round about, leaning on the obstacle as one goes. "Boygness" can, of course, take many forms—its amorphousness is one of its marvels. It can refer to religion, the demands of social convention, the requirements imposed by authority, whether public or private—indeed, anything that serves as a substitute for independent personal decision and as a psychologically adequate excuse for avoiding such decision. Mrs. Alving in *Ghosts*, Rosmer, and Hedda Gabler are the clearest examples of this tendency.

Mrs. Alving is a character who faces the tragedy of realizing too late the moral necessity of existential responsibility. Her tragedy is greater than that of any of Ibsen's other characters because she is made to face the hopelessness of her situation directly and to realize her guilt. For Ibsen tragedy almost always comes from *not* doing. The sin is omission. To follow the Boyg is to go by the book, to lean for support, to obey authority, *to have faith in something outside oneself.* Mrs. Alving has done all of these things, having always listened to the voice of the Boyg emanating with all the overpowering force of false moral authority from Pastor Manders. Manders, as is, of course, inevitable in one of his profession, is totally dehumanized in the sense that his brain is an automatic reflex mechanism programmed by the intertwined laws of religion and society. He has not only lost the power of independent decision; he represents the actual negation of that power. In a world from which the supernatural dimension has been removed—more precisely, in a world that has been freed from the illusion of its existence—the nescience of Manders equates him with what was formerly called the diabolic. He is the modern Tempter, and whosoever takes the easy path of following his blandishments loses *this* life, which is now all that there is. Mrs. Alving's recognition of her fate and her culpability at the end is just as stark as Faust's, and of the same nature. Next to *A Doll's House* and *An Enemy of the People, Ghosts* is Ibsen's most straightforwardly didactic play. It is from these plays that he gained his reputation as a polemic artist, and it is these plays that have had the greatest influence on subsequent writers. In them Ibsen defined the trend of analytic drama through his insistence on the supremacy and responsibility of the individual and through his rejection of authority as a guide to the actions of his characters.

Ibsen's other later plays all speak of this same theme, only more indirectly. The play immediately following *An Enemy of the People, The Wild Duck,* is a turning point. Ibsen himself said in a letter to his publisher that the play differed from all his previous plays.[16] He was clearly conscious at the time of writing that he was experimenting with a style new to him, though he could not have known then that he was to find his experiment so successful that all his subsequent plays were marked by it. Briefly put, what Ibsen had discovered was that he could build a play around a central symbol with the action efflorescing from or rotating round this still, quiet, nuclear center. Symbols were, to be sure, nothing new to Ibsen, but previously they had appeared strung out, as it were, along the path of a traditional linear plot. The Boyg and the onion appear along the path that the plot of *Peer Gynt* covers, illuminating the inner subtextual meaning of the action and then fading away again, having set the action in a new context. But the play is about Peer Gynt, and the symbols are intended to clarify his character. The wild duck is the subject of the play to which it gives its name, and everything that happens in the play emanates from it and revolves around it. To compensate for this, the play has no distinctly visible protagonist. This is one of the aspects of the play that has puzzled critical interpretation most severely. All of the characters—Gregers Werle, Hjalmar Ekdal, Old Ekdal, Old Werle, Hedvig, Gina, Relling—that play important parts in the action are fully realized psychological portraits. Their function is not principally to serve as foils to the protagonist, as was the case in the earlier plays.

If *The Wild Duck* is a play built around a central symbol and if that central symbol is the animal that gives the play its name, the principal question in an interpretation of the play must be what it is, precisely, that the wild duck symbolizes. In the play the wild duck is wounded—crippled, in fact—and lives as queen of the attic in the Ekdal household in the midst of dusty Christmas trees, broken clocks, and old books, with chickens, rabbits, and pouter pigeons for its companions. The household is supported more or less surreptitiously by Old Werle, who seems to be motivated in his charity by a guilty conscience since it is strongly hinted that he is the real father of Hedvig and that he was more than casually involved in the crime that led to Old Ekdal's disgrace and imprisonment. After Hjalmar Ekdal married Old Werle's former mistress, Old Werle set him up in the photography business, and he now pays Old Ekdal extravagant amounts for copying documents. He is also responsible for the wild duck's presence since he was the one who crippled it while hunting. It is the habit of wild ducks when wounded, we are told, to dive to the bottom and entangle themselves in the reeds until they die. This particular duck, however, was rescued by Old Werle's retriever, who dived down and brought it up again. And now it lives a pampered existence in the Ekdals' artificial forest, fat and contented, its free and natural life forgotten. As Hjalmar says in one of the play's many pregnant lines, "Well, she's been in there so long now that she's forgotten what it's like to live the life she was born for; that's the whole trick."[17]

Ibsen may have changed his technique, but his preoccupations remained the same. He was still as much as ever concerned with the necessity of facing up to the problems of life and making independent decisions about them. The need to analyze and dissect, to strive for self-reliance through acceptance of responsibility, and to free oneself from the horror of the human condition's innate inexplicability through the intensity of one's self-willed struggle against it rather than by succumbing to the narcosis of the time-honored received "truths" is always Ibsen's basic theme. The wild duck is a descendant of Peer Gynt's Boyg. It symbolizes the avoidance of reality that is for Ibsen the greatest crime. It is tempting to think of the wild duck's suicidal reaction to being wounded as an admirable trait, an uncompromising insistence on living its life on its own terms or not at all. But for Ibsen the "Give me liberty or give me death" attitude that the wild duck's reaction represents would surely have seemed merely infantile. It was a refusal to cope with the given conditions of life. What happened to the wild duck is not unusual: few, if any, go through life without suffering one or more crippling internal wounds. The transition to maturity that brings a realization of the nature of the human condition, the loss of innocence and illusion that even the first faint gropings of self-realization bring about are as crippling to our wills as the shotgun pellets to the wild duck's wing. Neither the wild duck nor Hedvig, who is its direct counterpart, ever come to that realization. Hedvig is at the far edge of childhood, about to face the possibility of achieving independence within herself: "Hedvig's at a difficult age just now," says Dr. Relling, "She's capable of getting up to anything. . . . Her voice is breaking." The wounding shock is too much for her, and she rejects life, shooting herself in the attic, which to her, her father, and her grandfather is as the reeds and the seaweed to the wild duck. For Old Ekdal the attic and his drunkenness are a refuge from the pain of his life. He too follows the path of the wild duck, as Old Werle makes clear when he says, "When [he] was released, he was a broken man, past help. There are some people in this world who sink to the bottom the moment they get a couple of pellets in their body, and never rise to the surface again."

Of Hjalmar it is almost too painful to speak. In him Ibsen has created the epitome of self-delusion and self-pity. Hjalmar never faces up to anything and never thinks of anything but himself. Though he too follows the wild duck's path in refusing to face life, he differs from it in his method, for he is the ultimate survivor who will keep on going round about through life, whining his self-justifications until they fade into his last self-pitying whimper. These three—Hedvig, Old Ekdal, and Hjalmar—are direct avatars of the wild duck inasmuch as their instinctive reaction to the problems of life is to dive down into the depths and die or accept a death in life.

Relling and Gregers Werle are the other two characters embodying the Ibsenian philosophy in this play, although they, too, embody it in a negative sense. The fatuous and mischievous Gregers, crippled by a necrophilous oedipal attachment to a hysteric, is a serious treatment of the comic Hilmar Tönnesen in *Pillars of Society* who goes around flaunting the "banner of the ideal." He is also, in his fanatical seriousness and devotion to his obsession, a secular, everyday version of Brand. Gregers' ideal is absolute truthfulness, which sounds good but is not. It is not good in the first place because it is an ideal. Ibsen did not believe in ideals, as can be amply demonstrated. Hilmar Tönnesen is a figure of farcical fun with his babble of carrying the "banner of the ideal." Dr. Stockmann, to whose supposed idealism Ibsen's creation of Gregers Werle is often said to be a corrective response, is not an idealist at all. Dr. Stockmann suffers from an excess of gullibility and enthusiasm, but he learns and changes, he makes decisions, possibly mistaken ones but his own, according to the circumstances. Unlike the pragmatic and existentially oriented doctor, Gregers worships a preset pantheon of conceptions. He is a true idealist—that is to say, he has faith and is consequently devoid of the ability to think for himself. The disaster that he brings on the Ekdal family is due to his trying to impose his own warped creed on them instead of allowing them to make their own decisions. The fact that without him no decisions of any kind would be made should be no concern of his. The Ekdals' life under anesthesia is their own tragedy, but it is a secondary one compared with that created by Gregers' determination to awaken them and make them see reality through *his* eyes.

Dr. Relling, whose commonsense denunciations of Gregers' obsessions and whose empathy with the Ekdals and with Molvik make him appear to be the *raisonneur* of the piece, is, if anything, worse than Gregers. He is not in any sense the spokesman for Ibsen's view that he has often been taken for. Seeing that his friend and neighbor Molvik is a guilt-ridden alcoholic, Relling, a physician, does nothing to alleviate his condition, but encourages it instead by convincing Molvik that he is not responsible for his actions and need feel no guilt because he is "diabolic." Seeing that Hjalmar is a self-indulgent and conceited simpleton who thinks photography is beneath him, Relling encourages him to believe that he will reform the profession with a great invention. He builds castles in the air for Molvik and Hjalmar and ensconces them on vaporous thrones there, fortifying their crippling disabilities and turning them into fake virtues. Relling substitutes fantasy for lethargy and guilt, and so obscures the possibility of self-consciousness which alone can be the salvation of the human animal in a world where fantasies have become crippling and prefabricated ideals have become out-of-date. And so all of these characters in one way or another resemble the wild duck, which symbolizes an attitude to life they all share, in that they choose death or the death in life that comes from going round about. Ibsen, wishing to show the necessity for self-creation and striving, showed the disastrous results of doing the opposite. From this play on, with the sole exception of the comparatively feeble *The Lady from the Sea*, Ibsen was to concentrate relentlessly on the failure to make existential choices that is the hallmark of those subjugated to the Boyg.

Ibsen's next two plays, *Rosmersholm* and *Hedda Gabler,* both ended with the protagonists diving down into the weeds and holding fast like the wild duck—literally in the former play. Rebecca and Rosmer walk into the millstream together at the end of the play, just as Rosmer's wife had done earlier, before the opening of the play's action. Logic led Ibsen astray when he wrote this dramatically and psychologically incredible ending: taken literally, as a realistic ending to a realistic play, Rebecca's and Rosmer's suicide can be interpreted only as an act of madness, a condition inconsistent with their behavior during the course of the play. But as a symbolic death in penance for their existential impotence the suicide makes perfect sense. It is as blindly desperate an act as the wild duck's dive to the bottom, for, like the animal, the two protagonists cannot face the changed conditions of their lives. Ibsen was fond of creating characters who reacted differently to the same problems; and so there is a strong bond between Rosmer and Dr. Stockmann. Both men feel they have a clear mission that has devolved on them because of their intellectual superiority and their position in the community. Rosmer, however, lacks that streak of recklessness and self-confidence that enables Dr. Stockmann to make the decision to take the necessary action. Their differing social backgrounds may have something to do with this too. Dr. Stockmann comes from the professional middle class and has worked his way up by his own efforts; Rosmer is depicted, to some extent at least, as the end product of a debilitated hereditary upper class who feels himself helpless to cast off the weight of tradition. His action in unfrocking himself seems to have exhausted his energies, and his finely honed sense of morbid guilt is exacerbated by the latent possibilities of his relationship with Rebecca. Together with the threats of his brother-in-law, Kroll, a close relative of Peter Stockmann in character, all these things combine to paralyze his powers of decision and drive him to the ultimate act of going "round about": suicide.

Hedda Gabler, of course, does nothing but go "round about" all her life. The Boyg is her God. Her marriage to the helpless ninny Tesman, a less repellent and more intelligent

version of Hjalmar Ekdal, is an escape from decision. It gives
her the safety she seeks and the death of emotional possibility
she craves, for she is as lamed in her emotional capacities by
her attachment to her dead father as Gregers Werle is by his
oedipal tie to his dead mother. Tesman is respectable, unde-
manding, adoring: the perfect haven from which to conduct
forays against the opposite sex with impunity. In strong contrast to Hedda, Ibsen created Thea Elvsted, her old school-
mate, unassuming yet determined and decisive, a Nora who
has successfully slammed the door behind her. Hedda sees her
own nullity compared with Thea and consequently hates her
with a corrosive savagery that dates back to their schooldays.
Hedda's great fear is scandal, and because of that fear she
never really lives—she lives only vicariously, at second hand.
She flirts with Judge Brack and with Eilert Loevborg, but
always keeps her pistols in reserve as a safety valve. Hedda's
tragedy is that she wants to live but dares not because she is
paralyzed by her ingrained respect for convention. Though
there is ample evidence for this in the text, Ibsen made his
intentions clear in his preliminary notes for the play, among
which we find "The play is to be about 'the insuperable' in the
longing and striving to defy convention, to defy what people
accept (including Hedda)" and "Loevborg has leanings
towards Bohemianism. Hedda is also attracted to it, but dares
not take the jump."[18] In the play itself Hedda reveals the ti-
midity and indecisiveness concealed behind her carefully constructed exterior when Thea Elvsted tells her she has left her
husband. Her first reaction is incredulity: "You mean you've
left your home for good?"—and when Thea calmly affirms
that she had no other choice, she says wonderingly, "But to do
it so openly!" That is the one thing that Hedda cannot understand: that Thea has not gone "round about." For Hedda life
consists of being shut up within a palisade, each stake of which
represents some artificial social custom; the excitement and
variety in her life come from peeking out between the stakes
with simulated boldness and quickly withdrawing again, waving her father's pistols menacingly, whenever the arrows of the
asocial savages outside come too close. Hedda, incapable of

taking action, experiences life vicariously, so that when Judge
Brack threatens the end of her "freedom" not to act she extin-
guishes what was never really there. Hedda commits suicide by
shooting herself in the head, but one feels that she could
equally well have killed herself by shooting her reflection in the
mirror.

   Rosmersholm and *Hedda Gabler* are not only plays about the
tragedy brought on by existential impotence. They represent a
turning point in Ibsen's work as well. Ever since *Peer Gynt* Ibsen
had been hammering away at the theme of the necessity for the
human being to make personal decisions based on the realities
of the situation and thus control his own destiny. All through
the great series of plays beginning with *Peer Gynt* up to and
including *Hedda Gabler* Ibsen had relentlessly fought the Boyg,
but in his last plays, beginning halfheartedly with *Rosmersholm*
and *Hedda Gabler,* a new theme supervenes and clearly becomes the principal element in his last four plays, *The Master
Builder, Little Eyolf, John Gabriel Borkman,* and *When We Dead
Awaken.* In a way it is as if he had got tired and had given up, as
if he had recognized that, except in a few cases, the Boyg was
too powerful to be defeated; and as if he had realized, perhaps
from his own life, that to defeat the Boyg involved the loss of
other and perhaps equally desirable aspects of life.

   Michael Meyer has pointed out that *Rosmersholm* "marks
Ibsen's final withdrawal as a playwright from the polemical
field. . . . Rosmer is the last of his characters to be caught up
and undermined by local politics; and Rebecca is the first of
those passionate but inhibited lovers who dominate the dark
plays of his final period."[19] Rosmer is, in fact, faced with two
dilemmas. He must decide whether to defy Kroll and the
Conservative faction in the local political conflicts, and he must
decide whether to give in to his attraction for Rebecca. The
dilemmas are interlocking inasmuch as there is some question
of the relationship between his suppressed feelings for Rebecca and his late wife's suicide. But the overall result is that
Rosmer fails in two ways, for he is capable of making an
existential decision neither about his intellectual life nor about
his emotional life. The overbearing weight of tradition pre-

vents him from publicly committing himself on the side he sincerely believes is right; and his ingrained moral scruples, which may well be subconscious evasions of reality, prevent him from committing himself to the passion offered by Rebecca. Hedda, too, is essentially a figure of thwarted passion. In her case there is, of course, no admixture of public interests. Hedda has no interests, except herself. Her isolation within herself is the reason for her failure as a human being. Isolation within the self is not necessarily bad when the self is interesting, but Hedda's is a barren wasteland. She has no interests, no talents; only her beauty and the longing for a sensual appreciation of life. Her tragedy is that her self-enslavement to tradition and convention prevents her from deciding to follow the lead of her deepest desires and instincts and causes her to experience Loevborg only vicariously; and later to submit herself to a life-stifling but respectable relationship with Tesman.

Emotional paralysis was to become the principal theme of the last plays and the principal sin of their protagonists. In all but one case—that of Alfred Allmers in *Little Eyolf*—it takes the form of sacrificing personal human relations to career.

It is, I believe, pointless to speculate on Ibsen's state of mind at the time he wrote his last plays. It is known that he had a succession of platonic relationships—mutual infatuations, really—with a series of extremely attractive and much younger women during this period. The ethereally passionate nature of these romantic relationships combined with the feeling that his analysis of the ills of the world and his prescription for curing them had fallen on deaf ears[20] may well have led him to feel that the true meaning of life lay in a one-to-one love relationship with the opposite sex on both the emotional and carnal levels. These plays, with their condemnations of blighted loves, can be seen as penitential apologia for Ibsen's own sublimations throughout a long life devoted single-mindedly to the pursuit of career and the betterment of his fellow man. Whatever the reason—and these biographical explanations, while most probably true, seem to me essentially irrelevant—the fact is that in his last plays, masterful though they are as theater and as psychological analysis, Ibsen had given up. He was no longer writing the drama of analysis with faith that the analysis would lead to solutions.

In Ibsen's late plays there is a sharp change in the quality of the women. From the domestic heroines of the earlier plays there is a sudden metamorphosis to "dream women" beneath whose idealized exteriors we can feel suppressed passions seething; they are still smoldering in the aged Ella and Irma of the last two plays. The sin of the protagonists is that they have not accepted what these women offered them. The one exception, of course, is Hedda, who combines male and female elements and has made herself inaccessible within herself.

Among the protagonists of the final plays Alfred Allmers is a case apart, as is that curious hybrid of a play, teetering on the borders of sentimental melodrama, disquisition play, and moral parable, in which he appears. Although Allmers' preoccupations are purely personal, his kinship is far more with Rosmer than with Solness, Borkman, and Rubek, the protagonists of the other final plays. Allmers is a man of leisure who plays at working; more precisely, he has become a man of leisure as a result of marrying Rita, an inordinately passionate woman who becomes totally infatuated with him. Allmers is never able to respond wholeheartedly to Rita, partially because of his suppressed desire for Asta, the woman he supposes to be his half-sister, and partially because of his constitutional incapacity for passionate feeling. Reversing the usual course of the late protagonists, he takes refuge in work on a book about human responsibility, a task for which he is as unfitted as he is for passion. *Little Eyolf* is the tragedy of a quintessentially unremarkable man cast into waters beyond his depth. Little Eyolf himself does not really figure in the play to which he gives his name except as a catalytic agent. His crippling fall off the table while his parents are making love renders Allmers impotent; his death enables his father to find a sort of peace in quiescence and a conscience-salving public service, while it renders incongruous his mother's passionate nature. The charitable work of helping the poor children of the village that they propose to themselves is a voluntary abdication from life, a reining in of feeling. Henceforth they will remain peacefully becalmed in the shallows that are the only waters a man of Allmers' stamp can survive in.

Unlike the rather effete Allmers, Solness in *The Master Builder* is an extremely virile man who has deliberately set his virility aside in favor of his ambition. The same may be said of John Gabriel Borkman and of Rubek in *When We Dead Awaken*. Solness' case, however, is far less straightforward than theirs. Both Borkman and Rubek have already died in every sense but the purely physical when their plays begin. As the title of Rubek's play hints, the subject of these two last plays is what happens when those who are spiritually dead are momentarily revivified by being brought face to face with the reminder of their lost opportunity and their wasted life in the desiccated person of the woman whose love they rejected for less worthy things. What happens is that they die physically as well. It is as if the sudden, unaccustomed fresh air that Borkman breathes after his years of petulant self-imprisonment or that Rubek breathes after his years of elaborating inhuman faces in stone is lethally alive. And the extinction is total, an extinction both of the false lives the men have led and of the true lives they might have led, for both Irma and Ella are themselves moribund. Ibsen reinforces his point of the supremacy of love by emphasizing that the careers of both men never were worthwhile. This is, of course, obvious in Borkman's case since he went to prison for his defalcations, but it is also clearly implied in Rubek's case. Rubek has apparently spent a lifetime working on a single statue, progressively despoiling its original perfection as his view of life became ever more cynical.

The Master Builder suffers from the same malaise as Borkman and Rubek, but Ibsen presented it more enigmatically in his case. Solness is clearly less culpable than his successors, an unconscious victim of his own psychic drives. While he is every bit as self-centered as Borkman and Rubek, he is far less callous than they are. Borkman's blindness to the plight of the people he has ruined in pursuit of his overriding dream of helping them by extracting the riches from the mines, his actual contempt for his victims, makes of him an impersonal—and impotent—magnet dreaming of drawing the ore from the depths.

Solness has none of this quality and is consequently guilt-ridden and much more human. He looks for things about which to feel guilty and for which to hate himself. Hence his ambiguousness about his professional success, which he justifies by inventing his supernatural "helpers and servers." He attributes the disaster that struck his family and at the same time served as the foundation of his professional fortune to these imaginary creatures. Although Solness, like most people, is the victim and/or the beneficiary of circumstances, his innate paranoia and the feelings of inferiority brought about by his suppressed knowledge of his dubious professional competence lead him to make up the "helpers and servers" as the responsible agents of his rise in the world and lead him also to make the wild and impulsive promise to Hilda ten years before the play opens. His promise to give her a kingdom, like his invention of the supernatural guardian spirits, is a manifestation of his need to prove that he is in control. His fear of heights as represented by towers is obviously a fear, or perhaps an outright acknowledgment, of sexual impotence. In keeping with Ibsen's basic existentialist philosophical orientation, failure *in* life is now what matters; and Solness, the glitteringly successful Master Builder, knows that he is and always has been a failure. The Broviks, father and son, are professionally more competent than he is, and he knows it and has cynically used them as the hidden foundation stones of his success. Similarly, his emotional life was barren long before the accident that destroyed his family and led to his success as a builder because he wished that the accident would happen in the conflict-ridden depths of his mind. Hilda Wangel's appearance and her faith in his greatness give him his chance, but it is too late for him to make full use of it. He frees himself of his guilt by giving young Brovik his opportunity, and thus making way for the younger generation he has feared so much, and by climbing the tower, where, before falling to his death, he lives his "short and happy" life, much like that of Francis Macomber in Ernest Hemingway's story.

Ibsen's last four plays are strange beasts in the dramatic landscape. In many ways they are superior to his earlier plays.

Certainly the depth of his psychological insight had increased, and the dissection of the protagonists is fascinating to watch. Nevertheless, they seem to me to represent a distinct falling-off from the thematic point of view. They are plays of psychological dissection *only,* lamenting in retrospect the lost opportunities of wasted lives. What is important is that these plays show discouragement. It is as if Ibsen felt that he had after all accomplished nothing. Discouragement is one of the inherent pitfalls in writing analytic drama. Unlike the fragmentational dramatists, who have accepted a particular view of the world, the analytic writers are dynamic. They feel the world's imperfection but do not look upon it as hopeless. It can be improved, and they feel that their function is to propose remedies. They see themselves, in other words, as social physicians. But, like the doctors in George Bernard Shaw's play, they too find themselves sooner or later in a dilemma. In Shaw's play the dilemma is whom to save when there is a limited supply of the healing drug. For the analytic writers the dilemma consists in their realization that there is some mysterious intrinsic factor in the moral makeup of the human being that prevents improvement beyond a certain point. There is, consequently, a tendency to retire from the fray, as Ibsen did, or to become a philosophical evangelist, as his principal disciple did.

In 1891 Shaw published *The Quintessence of Ibsenism,* in which he interprets Ibsen as a forerunner of the theater he himself intended to write. At the time he wrote his critical explication of Ibsen Shaw was still a year away from bringing out his first play, *Widowers' Houses.* When he did begin to write his plays, Shaw revealed himself as a typical analytic author. His first and third plays, *Widowers' Houses* and *Mrs. Warren's Profession,* dealt with absentee slum landlordism and the white-slave traffic, and performed the unlikely feat of basing excellent drama on these unpromising subjects. Vivie Warren in the latter play is Shaw's version of the Ibsenian woman, a Nora who slams the door before getting married. The play itself was intended to demonstrate that prostitution is a function not of morality or of innate depravity but of economics—and did so brilliantly and with a finality and dramatic force that enable it to hold the stage to this day. These two early plays, Shaw's own continuing development and perfection of the discussion play, and his habit of preceding the published versions of the plays with lengthy explanatory prefaces that few bother to read carefully and thoroughly, have led him to be considered the playwright as thinker par excellence. Except for those two early plays, however, Shaw was himself always ambiguous about his mission, and on the whole it would be more accurate to characterize him as "the playwright as dreamer." For Shaw saw early in his career that there was something incurable in the human being that made progress and betterment impossible. By 1903, when he wrote *Man and Superman,* he had reached a turning point in his thinking and had come to the conclusion that the human being must be transformed, not improved: transformed into a completely different creature—the Superman. He had decided that the change that was needed was one of kind, not one of degree. This change was to be accomplished by a magical power he called the Life Force, which he conceived of as an ineluctable evolutionary power that would inevitably transform mankind into a race of Supermen. Although he continued sporadically in his subsequent plays to hark back wistfully to the analytic qualities he had praised in Ibsen, Shaw had definitively turned to mysticism. His later plays are for the most part evangelistic exhortations covered with a glossy but transparent layer of rationalism. Like Ibsen, though much earlier and without realizing it, he had given up.

Shaw was a reluctant mystic. His instincts were all evidently the other way, and even in his latest works there are indications that he would have liked to have been able to remain the playwright he wrote about in *The Quintessence of Ibsenism.* Shaw understood what he himself was quite clearly when he wrote in the Epistle Dedicatory to *Man and Superman:* ". . . my conscience is the genuine pulpit article; it annoys me to see people comfortable when they ought to be uncomfortable; and I insist on making them think in order to bring them to conviction of sin. If you dont like my preaching you must lump it. I really cannot help it."[21] Earlier, in 1898, in the preface to *Plays Unpleasant,* he had explained what the burden of his preaching was to be: "I had no taste for what is called popular art, no respect for popular morality, no belief in popular religion, no admiration for popular heroics. As an Irishman I could pretend to patriotism neither for the country I had abandoned nor the country that had ruined it. As a humane person I detested violence and slaughter, whether in war, sport, or the butcher's yard. I was a Socialist, detesting our anarchical scramble for money, and believing in equality as the only possible permanent basis of social organization, discipline, subordination, good manners, and selection of fit persons for high functions."[22] Shaw clearly never fully understood that he had moved away from this description of himself. He continued to believe that he was presenting rational analyses of the world in his plays and prefaces and proposing remedies. And, indeed, he combined the two. In *The Doctor's Dilemma* (1906), for example, he combined analytic and what is best termed magical drama since it concerns limited, precisely defined, and attainable aims, like *Widowers' Houses* and *Mrs. Warren's Profession*, as well as wishful prescriptions for cosmic metamorphoses. On the one hand, there is the comic rogues' gallery of quack doctors who manage to be both sincere and cynical at the same time, admiring each other's methods for all the world like a group of conjurers admiring each other's acts; on the other, there is Louis Dubedat, the Artist/Superman contemptuously using them and everybody else in the name of the higher "morality" of his art.

The Doctor's Dilemma presents precisely the ambiguity that marked Shaw at this point of his career. Shaw was as much an inheritor of postrevolutionary nineteenth-century rationalism as Ibsen was, but he never lost the longing for the faith in an absolute. During the early part of his career the rationalist attitude was in the ascendant, but even then a wistful regret at the death of religion could be sensed as an undercurrent in his writing, just as later a stubborn hold on the materialistic values of his youth keeps rearing up like an isolated outcropping of solid rock in the shifting morass of uncertainty. Thus the lengthy preface to *The Doctor's Dilemma,* written seven years after *Man and Superman,* the drama that marked the turning point in his philosophical outlook, consists of a precise and reasoned dissection of current medical practice from the scientific, the economic, and the sociological points of view and recommends socialized medicine as the only answer to the inequities inherent in a capitalistic medical system where diseases are supplied in direct proportion to the growth of demand for remedies. At this stage he was still able to formulate as classic an example of the creed of analytic drama as ". . . when a habit of thought is silly it only needs steady treatment by ridicule from sensible and witty people to be put out of countenance and perish."[23] But the real cause of Shaw's essential dubiousness about rational solutions was that, except in the plays directly influenced by Ibsen, he never shared Ibsen's basic faith in human nature. He was never, like Ibsen, an existentialist. He never believed in the possibility of social or personal improvement through the independent decision of the individual. We think of characters like Trench, Vivie Warren, and Captain Bluntschli as prototypical Shavian characters, but they are not. They are thoroughly atypical from the essential Shavian point of view, being clever imitations of Ibsenian characters. Shaw himself was evidently not clearly aware of the change taking place in his concept of character, of his drifting away from the self-created Ibsenian character. In the Epistle Dedicatory to *Man and Superman* he criticizes Shakespeare and Dickens for creating characters that were puppets that needed "some artificial external stimulus" to make them work; of Shakespeare's characters specifically he says that all his "projections of the deepest humanity he knew have the same defect . . . their actions are forced on them from without." But this is precisely what may be said of Shaw's own characters. As far as their words are concerned, they are mouthpieces for Shaw's own views; as far as characterization is concerned, they are, with few exceptions (practically the whole cast of *Pygmalion,* for example), puppets moved by the postulated instinctive drive that Shaw called the Life Force.

The Life Force was Shaw's substitute for God. Its invention and explication were at once Shaw's most brilliant sustained intellectual achievement and the cause of his ultimate failure as a thinker. Unlike the existential thinker Ibsen, Shaw had no faith in the human being and adduced a good deal of perfectly valid evidence to back up his point of view. The only logical responses to a lack of faith in the human being's capacity for improvement are a stubborn optimism or despair. Shaw could not bring himself to apply the former to the human being as presently constituted and had an innate aversion to the latter. His solution was his own version of the illogical leap of religious faith: an impersonal cosmic force to replace the obviously shopworn and childishly insufficient traditional personal Judeo-Christian God. What is important in judging Shaw as a thinker is to realize that there is no more reason for postulating the one than the other. Shaw, just as much as any more orthodox religious thinker, sought solutions external to the mind of the human being; just as much as any more traditional theologian he regressed from the physical to the metaphysical, from positivism to mysticism. Nor did Shaw's leap make any more sense than the theologian's: the abyss he crossed had depths as murky and an opposite side as shiftily amorphous as the more traditional religious thinker's. Since he could not believe any longer in the sedulously presented fairy-tale atmosphere of direct supernatural intercession in the creation of the universe and in the management of everyday affairs, since he clearly perceived that the common man's theology was the intellectual's twaddle, and since, furthermore, he recognized that it had everything to do with the politicoeconomic subjugation of the majority and nothing at all to do with the undefined and undefinable "salvation" it pretended to be concerned with, he replaced it with a system that was at once more humane, more disinterested, and more impersonal. The traditional Unmoved Mover, First Cause, Supreme Godhead, or whatever impressive name was given to the concept whose concrete existence was assumed to have been established by the puerilities of ontological proof or of schizoid hallucination had been nothing more, really, than a vision of a village cacique, a backwoods county sheriff, or a banana-republic caudillo raised to the nth degree. His (Its?) purpose had been to transmit to mankind a set of rules of behavior that would assure its docility toward His (Its?) messengers and their sponsors or hangers-on. Shaw had the humanity to perceive that this was exactly the opposite of what was needed. If mankind was unable, as he believed, to save itself, it had to be saved by an external agency that was progressive rather than static, and expansive rather than repressive. Since, furthermore, man was incapable of significant permanent improvement, he would have to be changed in kind and not merely in degree. He would have to be transformed into a new and different kind of being altogether. Shaw, following Lamarck principally, envisioned this as coming about through an unconscious effort of the will that would eventually transform mankind into a race of Supermen and Superwomen through the creative evolution of the Life Force working instinctively in the eugenically procreative sex drive of woman.

Shaw had not conjured this metaphysical formulation ready-made out of thin air. As he saw it, the proof of the Superman's viability was that he had already appeared several times in history as an isolated freak of nature in the persons, for example, of the great artists and writers. This belief also accounts for Shaw's excessive admiration of such historical figures as Napoleon and Caesar, whose characters he recreated in his plays with a cavalier disregard for historical accuracy and a resolute insistence on keeping moral blinkers clapped tightly to his eyes. Later on, Joan of Arc is metamorphosed into an early Renaissance Ibsenian heroine; and finished models of the new Superrace are created in figures such as the Ancients in *Back to Methuselah* and Pra and Prola in *The Simpleton of the Unexpected Isles*. In Shaw's case, in short, despair had the curious and unusual effect of stimulating inventiveness, causing him to produce a modern theology that differed from the old one in being cleansed of cant, devoid of dogma, and unencumbered by God.

What had happened to Shaw? What caused the faithful Ibsenite believer in human progress, the devoted Fabian believer in political gradualism to turn first to a neoreligious evangelism and later to a reluctant flirtation with authoritarianism? William Irvine came as close to an explanation of the change in Shaw's thinking as anyone when he suggested that Shaw "was always a little too much impressed by recent events."[24] In the interval between his first play and *Man and Superman* in 1903 the Boer War, a triumph of yellow-press jingoistic propaganda, had been fought. The progress in education and in democratic responsibility that Shaw had advocated as a Fabian and the trust in individual improvement that he had believed in as an Ibsenite had proved hollow. The mass of his fellow citizens was revealed to Shaw as an atavistic pack ready to cast off its training and go baying in full cry after the first enterprising and ambitious lead dog to come along. It was the disillusionment brought on by the events of the late nineties that caused Shaw to write (in the Epistle Dedicatory to *Man and Superman*) that he had no illusions left about education, progress, "and so forth." It was here, too, that he formulated the attitude that was to characterize the principal trend of his thought in the plays that were to come:

> Any pamphleteer can shew the way to better things; but when there is no will there is no way. My nurse was fond of remarking that you cannot make a silk purse of a sow's ear; and the more I see of the efforts of our churches and universities and literary sages to raise the mass above its own level, the more convinced I am that my nurse was right. Progress can do nothing but make the most of us all as we are, and that most would clearly not be enough even if those who are already raised out of the lowest abysses would allow the others a chance. . . . We must either breed political capacity or be ruined by Democracy, which was forced on us by the failure of the older alternatives. Yet if Despotism failed only for want of a capable benevolent despot, what chance has Democracy, which requires a whole population of capable voters: that is, of political critics who, if they cannot govern in person for lack of spare energy or specific talent for administration, can at least recognize and appreciate capacity and benevolence in others, and so govern through capably benevolent representatives? Where are such voters to be found today? Nowhere.

Man and Superman was characterized by Shaw himself as a
play for philosophers about Don Juan in the philosophic sense.
In this sense, Shaw tells us, also in the Epistle Dedicatory, Don
Juan is a man who "follows his own instincts without regard to
the . . . law; and therefore, whilst gaining the ardent sympathy
of our rebellious instincts . . . finds himself in mortal conflict
with existing institutions, and defends himself by fraud and
force as unscrupulously as a farmer defends his crops . . .
against vermin." That is an excellent description of the Ibsenian protagonist, and indeed Shaw points out very acutely that
Nora is a version of what he calls the philosophic Don Juan in
skirts: "Don Juan had changed his sex and become Doña
Juana, breaking out of the Doll's House and asserting herself
as an individual instead of a mere item in a moral pageant." It
is, however, not in the least a description of Shaw's hero, John
Tanner, whom Shaw, with acute self-perception, modeled
physically on himself. Tanner is a man driven to talk and write
brilliantly but ineffectually. He is a man in the grip of the Life
Force, which uses him for its own end: the improvement of the
race through his union with the woman possessed of the Earth
Mother instinct. Tanner's brilliance and the dissemination of
his ideas are useless in themselves: they are only an indication
that he will be eugenically procreative, that he is one of the
seeds from which, after generations of refinement, will sprout
the Superman. Tanner, like his creator, is fully conscious of
this, as he shows when he says at the end of the play, after the
trap has been sprung, "I solemnly say that I am not a happy
man. Ann looks happy; but she is only triumphant, successful,
victorious." Adolphus Cusins in *Major Barbara,* another potential seed for the Superman, never consciously realizes this, but
Shaw reveals his function in a stage direction: "By the operation of some instinct which is not merciful enough to blind him
with the illusions of love, he is obstinately bent on marrying
Barbara."

The Superman that is to come will not be revealed fully until
Shaw describes his vision of him in *Back to Methuselah,* but some
of nature's imperfect trial attempts appear in earlier Shaw
plays. Caesar, trial run for the political Superman, is one of

them, as is Napoleon; Louis Dubedat, trial run for the artistic Superman, is another. The artist as Superman was one of Shaw's central conceptions. Dubedat in *The Doctor's Dilemma* is in every conventional sense a thoroughly unpleasant young man, totally amoral, mendacious, sly, and corrupt; but he has the true artist's vocation. In the context of Shaw's moral system his artistic creed redeems him, though it would not redeem a lesser man. Shaw portrayed him as a worthy heir of Michelangelo, Velázquez, and Rembrandt, his gods; and when he asserts his faith in "the might of design, the mystery of color, the redemption of all things by Beauty everlasting, and the message of Art" Dubedat is justified. The true artist, Tanner tells us, "will let his wife starve, his children go barefoot, his mother drudge for her living at seventy, sooner than work at anything but his art." And he is justified in doing so because he contributes his share to the transformation of the race into the Superman as surely as the woman with her procreative instinct does: ". . . the artist's work is to show us ourselves as we really are. Our minds are nothing but this knowledge of ourselves; and he who adds a jot to such knowledge creates new mind as surely as any woman creates new men."

The Superman, Shaw felt, would come about through the artist and the naturally superior political leader created gradually by the subconscious will working through the sex instinct. The concept of the naturally superior political leader caused him to take some extraordinarily unfortunate positions later in life when, again "a little too much impressed by recent events," he interpreted Russian Communism as a step on the path to a better race. A belief in the bankruptcy of conventional morality and in the necessity for a new one can lead one into pronouncing insanely exaggerated moral grotesqueries with no consciousness of having any but the most humanitarian intentions.

One of the necessary conditions for the advent of the Superman was the lengthening of human life. Another was the radical extirpation of the hypocritical cant that served to characterize and define the present state of society. These were to be Shaw's most important philosophical points in his subsequent plays. Both originated in *Man and Superman,* Shaw's philosophical watershed, as did the expression of the subconscious will through sex, which was the main point of the play.

Near the beginning of the hell scene Don Juan is accosted by Doña Ana de Ulloa, who has just died at the age of seventy-seven. Since she has changed from time to eternity she can be whatever age she wishes as far as her external appearance is concerned, Don Juan tells her: "You are no more 77 than you are 7 or 17 or 27." In life, he reminds her, outward appearances lie, and one is actually younger when one is old than one was in one's youth: "Consider, Señora: when you were 70, were you really older underneath your wrinkles and your grey hairs than when you were 30?" "No, younger: at 30 I was a fool. . . ." "You see, Señora, the look was only an illusion. Your wrinkles lied, just as the plump smooth skin of many a stupid girl of 17, with heavy spirits and decrepit ideas, lies about her age!" To say that Shaw goes to the heart of the human problem here is merely to say the obvious. To say that the human life span is uncertain and insufficiently long is to utter a truism. Shaw's contention that the ills of the human condition would be solved by an increase of the life span first to three hundred years and then to an enormously longer period is, almost amusingly, a reversion in the very midst of his despair-induced fantasizing to the confident optimism of his earlier years. Shaw has faith in man, after all, it turns out. All the ills of the world are due to man's being cut off before he can learn, before he can metamorphose himself into a qualitatively different and superior being. Man is already launched on the trajectory of perfection, but he suffers from a hitherto inevitable power failure before reaching his destination: the orbit of the Superman.

In *Back to Methuselah* (1920) Shaw worked out this attractive fantasy in full. Let it be emphasized, however, that drama based on fantasy, unless it be allegorical, is no longer analytical drama but magical drama; it analyzes nothing and proposes no solutions: instead it paints a picture of how nice everything would be if the problems were somehow solved. In *Back to Methuselah* Shaw is pulling rabbits out of hats. He differs from experienced cynics of the commercial theater like Barrie only in being himself under the spell of the illusion: Shaw thought the rabbits really were in the hat. The result was that the rabbits he pulled out of the hat were stuffed toy ones; but Shaw never noticed that.

In "The Gospel of the Brothers Barnabas" Shaw postulated as the first step along the path to the Superman the unconscious willing of a life span of three centuries on the part of certain individuals. The next great leap forward would then be when two of these select individuals mate two and a half or more centuries later. By far the most interesting part of *Back to Methuselah* is the last, set in A.D. 31,920. In this age people are hatched out of eggs fully formed mentally and physically at around seventeen years of age. They have affairs, play games, and generally behave in an utterly hedonistic manner for four or five years, after which they gradually become more and more serious. Then begins their long, slow transformation into one of the Ancients, for this advanced race of human beings does not die except by accident or by choice. They spend their time in the blissful contemplation of eternal abstract knowledge, free of all demands of the flesh. To Shaw, who once said that the greatest pleasure possible in life was the sensation of feeling one's own brain growing, this is a depiction of ultimate bliss. To the man who had John Tanner say that the only real passion is moral passion, the birth of which turns a child into a man, the atrophied bodies and elongated, swollen heads of the Ancients were the ultimate vision of beauty. The Ancients are not the end, for the possibilities of change are infinite; and at the end of the play Lilith, the earth spirit that *thought* creation into being, reappears to say, "It is enough that there is a beyond."

Shaw's bent for mysticism takes on a more humorous turn when he deals with the necessity for the elimination of hypocritical cant. Hell, Don Juan tells Doña Ana in *Man and Superman,* is the home of "honor, duty, justice, and the rest of the seven deadly virtues. All the wickedness on earth is done in their name . . ." In *The Simpleton of the Unexpected Isles* (1936) Shaw described an imaginary South Sea island on which, as a result of an experiment in eugenics conducted by some British colonialists and two natives, four children, two of each sex, have been born. The children, half white and half native (the exact nature of the race to which Pra and Prola belong is never made clear), are excessively beautiful and completely empty-headed, capable only of parroting slogans. They represent Love, Pride, Heroism, and Empire. Shaw's fantasy is that Judgment Day takes place during the course of the play; and in fact a rather comic angel comes down to announce it. When he leaves, the four children—and what they represent—have simply disappeared. Indeed, they are as if they had never been, for even their parents experience some difficulty in remembering them. Judgment Day, the Angel had said, would mean the disappearance of all those who were useless appendages to society. Henceforth, everyone would have to contribute to the best of his ability. In the preface to this play and in the one to *On the Rocks* three years earlier Shaw had made his impatience with those who opposed what he conceived of as the inevitable development of society explicit by writing some curious and uncharacteristic passages about the necessity for the painless and impersonal annihilation of people who were trying to subvert society.

The Simpleton of the Unexpected Isles is as perfect an example of magical drama as one could wish—or not wish—to see. How nice it would be, Shaw seems to be saying, if Love, Pride, Heroism, and Empire would simply disappear! How wonderful if the false ideals Ibsen fought against would just cease to exist without the individual's having to make the effort of extirpating them himself! Shaw was indulging himself in the fantasy of waving his magician's wand and ordering everything to flow back into Pandora's Box. Any responsible critic must be aware that writing in itself is an act of magic. The writer has it in his power to write anything—that is to say, to imagine anything as done. Anyone who has ever done any imaginative writing at all will recognize the feeling of illimit-able power that comes over the writer—for the writer is liter-ally a God who has it in his power to create new worlds peopled by characters made in his own image or in any other image that he pleases. Megalomania is the writer's endemic plague. It is

only with the greatest self-restraint—the test of true artistry—
that the writer can keep his creations within the dry dock of
reality, as Ibsen did. Without that restraint he plows into the
deep waters of fantasy and becomes engulfed in the waves of
his wishful imaginings, as Shaw did. Shaw had, in fact, become
a utopian. What is not generally recognized is that Utopianism
is born of despair. That better—and, in fact, eternally unattainable—world of Utopia, of heaven, of Nirvana, of the
classless Communist society, of the Kingdom of Heaven on
Earth when the lion shall lie down with the lamb is the imaginative refuge of those who cannot bear reality anymore, who see
no way to use it as a base for improvement, and who cannot
resign themselves to a life without hope that can end only in a
personal chemical disintegration and an endless repetition of
the same vapid senselessness in future generations. Utopia is
no easy thing to attain, however; and despair can make one
callous. Shaw was temperamentally unfitted to retire into the
existential individuality into which Camus' despair later led
him. Like all utopians, he combined practical despair with
visionary optimism; and pursued that vision with fanatical
idealism. The irony of Shaw's career is that he turned into a
parody of the Ibsenian idealist. Not content to wave the banner
of the ideal, he converted it into a pikestaff to stave in the heads
of his opponents. The theatrical good humor of *The Simpleton*,
with its comic angel announcing Judgment Day, and of *On the
Rocks*, with its good-fairy healer come to soothe the Prime
Minister's cares, is belied by their curious and ambiguous
prefaces.

The first section of the preface to *On the Rocks* is entitled
"Extermination" and ends with the sentence "Extermination
must be put on a scientific basis if it is ever to be carried out
humanely and *apologetically* as well as thoroughly."[25] One critic
has suggested that Shaw was practicing Swiftian irony here and
should properly have entitled the preface "A Modest Proposal
for the Extermination of the Politically Irresponsible" and that
the apparent callousness of the opening passages is belied by
the "moving plea . . . for the sacredness of criticism" at the end
of the preface.[26] The interpretation is understandable but in-

genuous. It is hard to think of Shaw, who was in so many respects the immaculate humanitarian, advocating the mass extermination of selected hordes of his fellow human beings. But the virulence engendered by disillusionment must not be underestimated: behind the mask of the idealist, as Shaw himself pointed out as far back as 1891 in *The Quintessence of Ibsenism,* lurks the fanatic. Furthermore, the comparison with Swift is an exaggeration. Swift advocated cannibalism for economic reasons, a proposition that cannot be taken seriously on a realistic level. Shaw advocated extermination for political reasons, a proposition that had in his own time been put into practice without the slightest moral compunction; and had throughout history been put into practice with enthusiastic fervor for religious reasons. Historically, indeed, extermination (or, to give it its modern technological name, genocide) has always been a means for moral uplift. Though he was an atheist by the standards of formal religion, Shaw had always been fascinated by the subject of religion and wrote about it continuously throughout his career, taking it seriously as a sincere, if mistaken, attempt to understand the nature of life and postulate an absolute truth. Unlike most atheists, Shaw never rejected religion outright as a deliberate perversion of observable fact and an ignoble degradation of the integrity of each human being's search for its own definition. Indeed, Shaw created his own religion with the impersonal and unerring Life Force substituting for the untidily temperamental God of the Scriptures. Life Force or God, however, psychologically the effect is the same: man is seen as object instead of as subject. To see man as an object is to be predisposed to treat him as one. Hence it is no surprise to find Shaw writing with admiration of the Russian experiment in extermination. Both in the preface to *On the Rocks*[27] and in the one to *The Simpleton of the Unexpected Isles*[28] Shaw speaks admiringly of the Russian official (identified as Djerjinsky, the founder of the Cheka, in the latter preface) who was obliged to go around shooting the stationmasters of various railway stations because they had ignored his directions for increasing the efficiency of the state railway system. Shaw, indeed, attributes the creation of the Russian secret police to the fact that Djerjinsky was a naturally timid and merciful man who didn't like shooting people himself.[29] The socially uncooperative stationmasters must be shot—"humanely and apologetically," to be sure—because they are obstructing the currently accepted form of social progress; and their extermination is morally justifiable for, as Shaw put it, "the essential justification for extermination . . . is always incorrigible social incompatibility and nothing else."[30] In the dialogue between Jesus and Pilate that Shaw inserted into the preface to *On the Rocks* Pilate is portrayed as reluctantly condemning Jesus because the latter simply refuses to conform to the currently acceptable ways of doing things. Shaw is not arguing that Pilate's view was right and Jesus' wrong. He was simply pointing out that one who goes as sharply against the social grain as Jesus did can expect no better treatment than he received.

Progress can come about only through criticism, of course; and it is for this reason that Shaw concluded the preface to *On the Rocks* with his apparently self-contradictory plea for the sacredness of dissent. But the privilege of criticism was to be reserved for those who were on the right path, lest they be martyred by an inflexible and reactionary system, as Jesus was. "Now the heretic in Russia . . . is an active, violent, venomous saboteur . . . [because of] his fanatical hatred of a system which makes it impossible for him to become a gentleman. Toleration is impossible: the heretic-saboteur will not tolerate the State religion; consequently, the State could not tolerate him even if it wanted to."[31] That the burden of Shaw's remarks in the prefaces to *On the Rocks* and *The Simpleton* is not "a moving plea . . . for the sacredness of criticism" is made explicit in the closing paragraph of the former: "In the meantime [until "standards of worth get established and known by practice"] the terror will act as a sort of social conscience which is dangerously lacking at present and which none of our model educational establishments ever dreams of inculcating."[32] In his significantly entitled lecture "In Praise of Guy Fawkes," delivered in 1932 for the Fabian Society, Shaw had taken up the same theme without the faintest tinge of anything that could be taken for irony:

> You have to look final issues in the face. There comes a time in all human society when there is a certain constitution of society which a number of people are determined to maintain and a number of people are determined to overthrow. Both have the conviction that the whole future of the world and civilization depends (a) on its being maintained, (b) on its being overthrown. The only way in which it can finally be settled, it seems to me, is by one party killing the other to the extent that may be necessary to convince the rest that they will be killed if they do not surrender. I do not think there is any use in burking that sort of fact by cherishing the old Liberal illusion that fundamental reforms can be effected by votes in Parliament. . . . There is only one way . . . and that is to get at the children and raise a new generation educated as Socialists. That would give you a Socialist movement in the country overwhelming enough to put out of countenance the propertied resistance. Without that the thing will be done by the forcible determination of a resolute minority, as it has been done in Italy and Russia. . . .
>
> Well, ladies and gentlemen, take my advice and do not try to defer the catastrophe. Do everything you can to bring it about, but do your best to let it be done in as gentlemanly a manner as possible.[33]

A gentlemanly catastrophe is a contradiction in terms. The phraseology is an indication of the slough of fantasy into which Shaw had fallen. The bumbling, amiable Angel who came to sweep away Love, Pride, Heroism, and Empire in *The Simpleton of the Unexpected Isles* is a gentlemanly exterminator, but when converted into the reality about which Shaw did not want to think he becomes the fire and sword of modern genocidal extermination. He represents Shaw's final failure as a productive thinker.

Bertolt Brecht's case is more complex. It is hard to imagine that Shaw was totally unaware of his turn to apocalyptic thinking with his faith in the inevitability of Lamarckian evolution and his creation of a "religion" based on the workings of an irresistible yet unconscious human will. Brecht, on the other hand, never succumbed to this sort of mysticism born of sublimated despair. He retained his belief in analytic philosophy and in the ability of dialectics to solve problems. Analytic drama is dialectical in structure, containing thesis, antithesis, and synthesis. In Ibsen and in some of Brecht this synthesis is implied or left up to the decision of the audience. This is true, also, of Shaw's early, or Ibsenian, phase. In Shaw's later phase, magical drama, the antithesis is left out. The characteristic of magical drama is that the playwright leaps straight from thesis to synthesis, which is presented to the audience as a fait accompli. Thus, in *Man and Superman* Shaw makes the leap from the thesis of the supremacy of woman in intersexual relations through the possession of the Life Force, to the synthesis of the possibility of the Superman. In *Back to Methuselah* he goes from the thesis of the inadequacy of the human life span directly to the synthesis of a three-century life span and finally a theoretically eternal life span. The necessary logically bridging antithesis is entirely lacking in these and later Shavian plays. Brecht does not fall into this error, though he does occasionally wander into the equally damaging one of presenting the synthesis in a sedulously inculcating manner in his *Lehrstück* period. Nevertheless, as we shall see in his great quartet of plays written in exile—*Mother Courage, The Good Woman of Sezuan, Galileo,* and *The Caucasian Chalk Circle*—Brecht produced a curious perversion of the analytic play, retaining its form but twisting and distorting its philosophy out of all recognition.

Brecht's earliest plays, written before his complete commitment to Communism, were *Baal, Drums in the Night,* and *In the Jungle of the Cities.* These plays do not in the least resemble the plays on which Brecht's reputation is based, but they are of interest in revealing the basic aspect of Brecht's thought. Brecht probably never changed his basic outlook on life, despite the apparent differences between the two stages of his intellectual development. As plays these early works are poor stuff indeed, juvenilia of the worst kind—disjointed in structure, clumsy in language, and poor in stagecraft. They are by no means the beginning of a new era in dramatic art, as one critic has maintained. The same critic has suggested, a good deal more sensibly, that "If . . . a good play amounts finally to a particular vision of life seen as a whole, then this play [*Baal*] is a vision of life as an inferno."[34] The same might be said of the other two early plays, as well as of Brecht's fourth play, *A Man's a Man.*

Stylistically, *Baal* is a parody of expressionism; thematically, it is a savage repudiation of conventional morality to the point of total nihilism. *Drums in the Night,* like so many other post–World War I German plays, is on the theme of the forgotten soldier returning from the war. Brecht sets the action in the midst of the Spartacus uprising of 1919 and has his protagonist refuse to join it in favor of the comforts of a bourgeois life. Brecht tried to explain this away later on by asserting that he intended his protagonist to be a portrait of a proto-Nazi, but the text does not support his claim. While Kragler, the protagonist, is not shown in a favorable light, no one else is either. The theme of the play is the uselessness of political action, and Kragler's solution is shown as being as worthwhile as any other—that is to say, of no worth at all.

In the Jungle of the Cities is a totally chaotic play. Its thesis is that pointless mutual enmity is the only possible, even faintly meaningful, form of human communication. Brecht did not, in fact, really begin to hit his stride stylistically until he wrote *A Man's a Man.* This play shows the first definite signs of the demonstrative, "epic" theater style that Brecht was to make his trademark. His subject here is the interchangeability of human character. The human personality does not exist except insofar as it is defined by its function in society. The protagonist is changed from a peaceful laborer into a ruthless fighting machine by the simple expedient of putting him into a uniform and giving him an identity card.

Had Brecht continued to write in the vein of his first four plays he would have become a typical fragmentational writer. His basic belief in these plays is lack of belief, rejection of society and of any intrinsic human qualities. He is the total nihilist in these plays. His attitude to life is succinctly summed up in a scene from *Baal.* A lumberjack named Teddy has just died, and the following exchange takes place:

> BAAL: . . . Teddy was generous. Teddy was easy to get on with. And of all this, one thing remains: that Teddy *was.*
> SECOND LUMBERJACK: I wonder where he is now?
> BAAL *(pointing to the dead man):* There.[35]

This ultramaterialistic viewpoint and its accompanying cynicism about the potentiality of the human being for self-improvement are what led Brecht paradoxically to the essentially religious orientation of Communism. His dissatisfaction with the society in which he lived and the blame that he felt capitalism must bear for the inequities of that society also undoubtedly led him in that direction. It was the materialistic and cynical attitude that brought Brecht to the belief that human impulses had to be channeled by external directives, by the application of a *theory* as to how people should behave; and thus to a philosophy that provided a teleological solution in nonmetaphysical terms. In *A Man's a Man* he had demonstrated that man had no fixed definition. He was malleable. There remained only the question of what he was to be molded into. Galy Gay, the protagonist of *A Man's a Man,* is molded in accordance with his—and man's—atavistic instincts into a fighting machine. The corollary to Brecht's proposition in the play is that a little more care and direction would have molded him into a useful member of a useful society as defined by any particular ideology. Given Brecht's materialism, the logical ideology for him to choose was Communism, which promised a paradise on earth in which classes would be eliminated and the economic hardships imposed by capitalism unknown. Like all those who have given up on the world and yet refuse to accept the reality that they see, Brecht adopted a religion and henceforth proceeded to espouse it with evangelistic fervor.

What had happened to Brecht was that he, too, had fallen into the trap of magical drama. Although he continued to write analytic drama formally, retaining its characteristic dialectical structure, he had adopted magical drama philosophically. It must be emphasized, however, that Brecht's version of magical drama was radically and qualitatively different from Shaw's. Shaw could not have been unaware that there was an element of faith—and, therefore, of mysticism—in his belief that man would evolve into Superman. Furthermore, the mere assertion that man must become Superman is an admission of despondency bordering on despair. Man per se can accomplish nothing, Shaw was saying. He must not merely get better: he must change in kind as well as in degree. Brecht, in thinking that man need only change in degree, need only get better, need only learn to act collectively in order to bring about the classless Arcadia was, paradoxically, more self-deluded than Shaw, for he never realized, as Shaw most certainly did, that an element of the intangible—indeed, of the indefinable—was a part of the formula for progress that he advocated. Shaw realized that he was operating in the ethereal stratosphere of wish-fulfillment fantasy when he postulated an ineluctable Life Force driving mankind from its protean ancestors through its present transitional phase to the lambent glory of the virtually disembodied, supernally cerebral Superrace. Shaw's attitude to reality is summed up in the surprise with which his two survivors—the maid and the curate from the "Gospel of the Brothers Barnabas" section—realize in *Back to Methuselah* that they of all people have been chosen by the Life Force to live three hundred years and advance humanity one step further on the road to the Superrace; Brecht's in the uncompromising "Q.E.D." that he appends to the demonstration of Galy Gay's metamorphosis in *A Man's a Man*.

The Measures Taken is a play typical of Brecht's middle period, written in the first flush of enthusiasm for the new religion he had adopted. The play deals with an inquest on a Communist infiltrator in China. A "Control Chorus" is the judge at the inquest, and the defendants are the four surviving returned infiltrators, who admit having shot their comrade and buried him in a lime pit. It is revealed that the dead man had repeatedly jeopardized the success of their mission by his tendency to let personal humanitarian considerations take precedence over the larger job at hand, which was to make propaganda and build up the influence of the party in the factories of Mukden. On one occasion he had protested against the brutality that overseers showed to coolies; on another he had prevented a worker from being unjustly arrested and possibly killed for distributing propaganda leaflets that he had himself passed out. As the other agitators point out, this helped neither the coolies nor the worker and instead aroused the vigilance of the authorities, thus making the further distribution of propaganda extremely difficult and hazardous. The dead agitator, in other words, had committed the crime of putting "his feelings above his understanding." Finally he revealed himself to the people as a Communist agitator, thus "blowing his cover," and all five had to flee. The dead agitator had to be overpowered by the others, and, since his injury was hampering their escape, he begged them to kill him, which they did. The "Control Chorus" absolves them from all blame and tells them they have done well because

> You have spread
> The teachings of the classics
> The ABC of communism:
> To the ignorant, instruction about their situation
> To the oppressed, class consciousness
> And to the class conscious, the experience of revolution.
> In yet another country the revolution advances
> In another land the ranks of the fighters are joined
> We agree to what you have done.[36]

The Measures Taken was designated by Brecht himself as a *Lehrstück*, a "learning play." It is a full dialectical analytic play inasmuch as it dissects the human situation and purports to present a solution to it. In form, consistent with its being a *Lehrstück*, it presents the thesis, which is taken for granted, of the misery of the human condition under capitalism; the antithesis, Communist teaching; and the synthesis, the utopian Communist state. But it should be noted and emphasized that it has also all the characteristics of a medieval morality play in the full religious sense of the term. The setting of the play is an inquisitorial trial conducted by the "Control Chorus," which has implicit power of life and death over the agitators and which is the apex of an explicitly accepted hierarchical order. The agitators clearly consider themselves as no more than machine cogs in function and as replaceable building blocks in importance. They are "Servants of Utopia" in exactly the same sense as missionaries are "Servants of God" and have the same sense of selfless dedication: only the ideal, never the individual, counts. Similarly, there is the reliance on the absolute, immutable authority of the Bible and the church fathers, here called the classic writers and the ABC of Communism: ". . . we bring the Chinese workers the teachings of the classic writers and the propagandists, the ABC of communism; . . . Marching forward, spreading the teaching of the communist classics: World Revolution."[37] Finally, there is the exemplary acceptance of martyrdom by the sinning agitator in search of redemption.

Brecht's other *Lehrstücke*, *The Exception and the Rule*, *The Yeasayer*, *The Naysayer*, and *The Mother*, the last-named adapted from Gorki's novel, are all written in this finger-wagging vein. Like the agitprop plays being written in the United States at about the same time (the 1930s) these plays suffer from the innate contempt of their writer for the working classes they purported to admire and for whom they were composed. They are "written down" as if to preliterate children, the writer tacitly assuming that the uneducated masses could not possibly understand anything more sophisticated. In dialectical terms, the synthesis is provided, the solution spoon-fed, since there is no confidence that the intended audiences have the brains to make up their own minds.

Had Brecht ceased to write after he had produced his *Lehrstücke* he would hardly be remembered at all today. It was only after fleeing Germany, when he had no immediate audience demanding a particular type of play, that he began to write the plays by which he is and will be remembered. These plays are for the most part parables in form and provide only thesis and antithesis, leaving the synthesis to the audience. This is not, of course, to say that these plays have no ideology—only that the synthesis is conveyed to the audience subtly, as in Ibsen, instead of being explicitly hammered in.

In most of the plays of his exile period Brecht expounds the pessimism that is so visible in his first four plays. The feelings that he had expressed then had been submerged during his *Lehrstück* period when he was espousing the orthodox Communist position with such devoted fervor. That fervor, however, was clearly never the expression of a firmly held belief. It seemed to partake more of the nature of an oasis of certainty for a man lost in a desert of irredeemable pessimism; but Brecht never rid himself of the suspicion that, like most oases, this one was a mirage too. The rigid "by the book" orthodoxy of his *Lehrstücke* makes them almost a parody of the form. Reading them, one has the feeling that Brecht wrote them in the same spirit as that of a Catholic convert who continues to doubt yet desperately wishes to believe and substitutes for sincerity a punctual saying of his offices and a rigid adherence to the prescribed fasts and penances. It seems clear from his later plays that Brecht's deep-rooted pessimism had been in no way attenuated.

In his great quartet of plays written in exile—*Mother Courage, The Good Woman of Sezuan, Galileo,* and *The Caucasian Chalk Circle*—Brecht developed his dramatic principles to their highest point. With his theatrical genius Brecht brought the genre of didactic drama to its apogee. The alienation effect he devised to facilitate the audience's emotional dissociation from the action in order to enable it to contemplate the intellectual significance of the play objectively and impersonally is and will remain one of the landmarks in the development of theatrical technique. As effective theatrical vehicles these plays must rank with the masterpieces of theatrical literature. Their intellectual value is, however, suspect. At first glance these plays, dialectical in form, appear to be analytical plays in the Ibsenian mode. Like Ibsen's middle-period plays, they appear to be tragedies of failure, of omission. On further examination, however, they appear to be not all that different from the overtly propagandistic *Lehrstücke*. By excising the pedantry that made the *Lehrstücke* so intellectually cloying, Brecht made these plays palatable to audiences who find the earlier plays offensive; but the ideas remain essentially the same. Brecht is still concerned with the establishment of a secular religion that substitutes the inevitable results of a putative social determinism for the inscrutable fiats of an omnipotent and presumably benevolent God. The only difference is that God has been desacralized and reconstituted as the juggernaut of social destiny.

We can see this process at work in *The Good Woman of Sezuan,* which is a parable about the impossibility of a moral existence under capitalism. In dialectical terms the thesis of the play is the state of society at present with its economic rapacity and its pretended reliance on the moral code of religion; its antithesis is Shen-Te's selflessness and literal personification of the religious moral code; and its synthesis is her unwilling but necessary transformation into the heartless Shui-Ta. The implication that Brecht hopes his audience will draw is that the thesis must be changed in order to bring about a more satisfactory synthesis. Brecht's portrayal of the thesis is exaggeratedly polemical and debatable, but it is an accurate reflection of his own view of capitalistic society as being without any redeeming qualities. The antithesis and synthesis are similarly one-dimensional. Shen-Te is completely good—at first the traditional prostitute with a heart of gold, then the businesswoman as saint. Shui-Ta, her alter ego, is the stock figure of the heartless, grasping capitalist exaggerated to the limits of belief. Brecht's point is that the capitalistic system is itself so morally bankrupt that a person who actually lives in acordance with all the moral ideals to which the system pays lip service can survive only by converting herself into a monster who overtly negates those ideals. This brings Brecht to the central paradox of his play, which is that the moral person can do limited good and survive only by acting immorally in this system. In a capitalistic society no amount of self-determination (i.e., of analytic behavior) can overcome the pressure of social forces, seen by Brecht as an ineluctable collective deterministic stamping press. Brecht took the bold and radical step of completely

rejecting all the conventions of the realistic theater and con-
structing instead an abstract parable devoid of psychological
verisimilitude in a fairyland setting. Again, as in the plays of
the *Lehrstück* period, he has written a morality play, but this
time it is not "written down" to an audience for which he
subconsciously felt contempt. *The Good Woman of Sezuan* is a
play written for a mature audience that is given the choice of its
own conclusion. At the same time it must be noted that Brecht's
genius as a theatrical manipulator bamboozles us. *The Good
Woman of Sezuan* eliminates psychological verisimilitude and
substitutes attitudinizing; the characters represent different
points of view in a schematically simplified social structure,
their moves as rigidly plotted as those of chess pieces. The
belief in free will that is essential to the analytical view of life is
totally absent here. Brecht instead performs the virtually self-
contradictory philosophical and essentially religious feat of
asserting a belief in an optimistic determinism.

Mother Courage, too, is a curiously deceptive play, rendered
so by Brecht's theatrical genius. Actresses all over the world
have looked on the title role as a choice part. And so it is—up to
a point. It is a superb *theatrical* part with all sorts of opportunities for effective scenes; but it is a part that entirely lacks
dramatic complexity. Eric Bentley has declared that *"Mother
Courage is above all a philosopher, . . .* a person who likes to . . .
explain everything to everybody."[38] This seems to me to miss
an essential point and at the same time to guide us to an
understanding of why Brecht is so much less a universal playwright than Ibsen is. Dr. Stockmann may be said to be above all
a philosopher—though not by any means a particularly good
one. But, then, how many people are? Kroll in *Rosmersholm* is a
philosopher of sorts too—a worse one even than Dr. Stockmann, most people would say nowadays. He, too, feels im-
pelled to explain things to people. We cannot, however, assert
that Kroll's or Stockmann's explanations are Ibsen's. Kroll and
Stockmann, like all the creations of Ibsen's maturity, are fully
formed characters, recognizable human and social types who
are still with us. The same cannot be said of Mother Courage.
In one sense Bentley is right: she is a pure philosopher, much

more than Kroll or Stockmann; but, unlike them, she is not
rooted in reality. She is not still with us—has, in fact, never
been with us. And consequently her philosophizing is not
integral to her character, for that was created in order to
philosophize and is not rooted in the reality she is talking
about. The philosophy she espouses is not hers, the explanations she constantly gives to everybody are not hers. They are
Brecht's. Properly speaking, she is not a character in the cus-
tomarily accepted dramatic sense at all but a schematic stick
puppet functioning as a mouthpiece for the author. Mother
Courage never acts; she always reacts. Circumstances are the
real protagonists of this play. The same thing that can be said
of Shen-Te can be said of Mother Courage: she is a marionette
at the end of socioeconomic strings manipulated by the mysterious and malign forces of history. At the end of the play
Mother Courage has lost everything. Yoked to her cart like a
beast of burden, she carries on. Life—i.e., business—must go
on. And "life" and "business" will remain synonymous and will
continue to enslave the human spirit until the long-awaited
dawning of the classless paradise. But Mother Courage is not
the symbol of the defeat of the soulless system in which she and
we live. She is neither courageous, nor indomitable, nor admirable. She simply *is:* a creature on rails, so to speak, reacting to
necessity. The apparent indomitability of Mother Courage in
the final scene is ironic. She is no more indomitable than an ox
is. Like the ox, she does whatever she does because she has to
and because *she knows no other way.* The final scene should be
laughed at, though one might need a turn of mind as subtly
sardonic as Brecht's to do so with confidence. Mother Courage
is a plaything of social forces. She is a dupe who has neither
courage nor heroism: only instincts that have been warped by
the pressures of the wrong socioeconomic environment. She is
the quintessential victim, a dumb beast of burden on a tread-
mill to oblivion.

Both Shen-Te and Mother Courage are victims of deterministic circumstances over which they have no control, which
trample mindlessly on their feelings as human beings and
prevent them from even beginning to think of fulfilling them-

selves as individual entities. *The Caucasian Chalk Circle* is a more lighthearted play in which the heroine, Grusha, is fulfilled. Grusha knows what she wants and works out her own destiny so that at the end of the play she gets what she wants. She achieves all she has striven for. *But only because she is permitted to.* *The Caucasian Chalk Circle* is not only based on a fairy tale: it *is* a fairy tale. In it Brecht relaxes and spins a fantasy of what it will be like when the wished-for multimillennium arrives. A millennium of sorts has already arrived with the Russian victory in the Second World War, as we see in the tiresomely admonitory prologue where the fruit growers and the goat breeders are guided to an amicable solution on the best Benthamite principles by the benignly avuncular and subtly manipulative promptings of the Delegate of the State Reconstruction Commission, who plays the part taken by the mysterious Azdak, also an emissary from Higher Powers, in the fable.

In the play itself Brecht dramatizes a biblical parable to imply a socialist viewpoint. A baby is abandoned by its mother, who is more interested in saving her dresses. It is reluctantly taken care of and adopted by a servant girl during the rebellion that caused it to be abandoned by its fleeing mother, the wife of the overthrown governor. At the trial to determine who shall keep the child it is awarded to the servant girl who cared for it and not to the woman who gave it birth and therefore considers it her property. The decision of the trial is the synthesis to the thesis of the abandoned child and the antithesis of the servant girl's adoption of it. The implication, as the Reverend Morell puts it in Shaw's *Candida*, is that "We have no more right to consume happiness without producing it than to consume wealth without producing it."

The Caucasian Chalk Circle is a wish-fulfillment fantasy. While the play's dialectical structure clearly concerns the story of Grusha and the child, and while Grusha is clearly the protagonist, the play equally clearly rests on Azdak's somewhat elusive shoulders. The point of the play is that Grusha gets the child she has cared for and brought up; that is to say, things work out in the play the way they ought to work out. Justice triumphs. But how does it triumph? Through the idiosyncratic intervention of Azdak. And who is Azdak? Azdak appears only in part 2 of the play, which is entitled "The Story of the Judge," and totally dominates it from then on. He is introduced to us as being the Village Recorder, but he does not seem to make very much out of the job: he is dressed in rags, lives in a filthy hut in the woods, and supplements his diet by poaching. As a result of a complicated series of accidents, Azdak is appointed judge and begins to dispense justice in accordance with common sense rather than in accordance with the law or with expediency. For the two years or so that Azdak is in the judge's seat justice reigns in the land. Azdak's reign as judge is a skewed glimpse of the Golden Age to come. He is an emissary of that utopian era, but he is himself deliberately flawed by Brecht to show that he is not the personification of the ideal but is subservient to it. All human beings, indeed, are subservient to the abstract ideal in Brecht's Utopia—as they are in all Utopias. Azdak, who conceives that he has done wrong, albeit inadvertently, by sheltering the Grand Duke, denounces himself publicly and demands punishment in the best orthodox Communist fashion. He appears on the scene matter-of-factly enough, but he disappears in a manner that raises him to the superhuman level. After he has rendered the judgment of the chalk circle he orders a dance. The dance begins and "Azdak stands lost in thought. The dancers soon hide him from view. Occasionally he is seen, but less and less as more couples join the dance."[39] He vaporizes, for he is not a real but a mythical figure. The Story Teller ends the play by pointing the moral:

And after that evening Azdak disappeared and was not seen again.
The people of Grusinia did not forget him but long remembered
The period of his judging as a brief golden age
Almost an age of justice.

All the couples dance off. AZDAK *has disappeared.*

But you, you who have listened to the Story of the Chalk Circle,
Take note what men of old concluded:
That what there is shall go to those who are good for it,
Thus: the children to the motherly, that they prosper

The carts to good drivers, that they are driven well
And the valley to the waterers, that it bring forth fruit.[40]

The appearance of Azdak and his momentary Golden Age is
like the appearance of the prototypical Superpeople in Shaw—
the Caesars, the Joans, the Dubedats—who "prove" the possibility of evolution to a Superrace. Why should the wish-
fulfillment fantasy of the last part of *Back to Methuselah* not be
true? After all, we have had glimpses of Supermen before!
Why should the classless Utopia not be lurking in the future if
brief, prefiguring Golden Ages occur? The Azdaks and their
Golden Ages prove that a time will come when what Morell
says will be true, when we will be released from our chains in
the cave and see the "reality" outside. The comparison is not
vain: the similarities between Plato's Utopia and the Communist one, though unconscious, are profound. The dream of
enforced happiness and tranquillity leads to magical thought
in Brecht, as much as it did in Plato and Shaw.

Brecht is known today in English-speaking countries principally by *The Threepenny Opera*, *Mother Courage*, *The Caucasian
Chalk Circle*, *The Good Woman of Sezuan*, and *Galileo*. Of these
the last four were written in exile, and only the last named may
properly be said to be an analytical play. As might be expected
from one so accustomed to the facile paths of magical thinking
through his acceptance of an external ideology, Brecht's
attempt at writing an analytical play, while superbly successful
theatrically, tends to a considerable degree of philosophical
confusion. Part of this confusion is the result of Brecht's in-
veterate habit of rewriting his plays, which in the case of *Galileo*
resulted in three separate complete versions. The first version
was written in 1938; the second, dating from 1945, exists only
in English and was the translation credited to Charles Laugh-
ton, who worked on it with Brecht for the production in which
he played the lead; the third was a retranslation and adapta-
tion by Brecht for his own production at the Berliner En-
semble.

Brecht's original motivation for writing the life of Galileo in

1938 was the curious behavior of a large number of his fellow German intellectuals with respect to the Nazi regime. The curious aspect of their behavior from Brecht's point of view was the failure to protest. Both collaboration and quiescence were prevalent reactions among the intelligentsia. Brecht's reaction was to write a play about a man who *appeared* to be quiescent but was in fact secretly undermining the regime. In this version Galileo is vindicated and, indeed, triumphs when he hands Andrea the extra manuscript of the *Discorsi* to smuggle over the border to freer lands. The extra copy has been laboriously written from memory at night at the cost of much of Galileo's remaining eyesight and sardonically concealed in a globe of the world with a fine contempt for his jailers' capacity for symbolic thought.

The second version reflects Brecht's reaction to the dropping of the Hiroshima bomb. As Brecht put it in his notes to the play, "The biography of the founder of modern physics assumed a different meaning overnight." He goes on to say that only very few alterations, none of them structural, were necessary.[41] Most of the changes came in the penultimate scene where Galileo gives Andrea the *Discorsi* to smuggle out. In the original version the scene is Galileo's triumph: he has succeeded in duping the authorities and vindicating himself. In the revised version Galileo excoriates himself for his cowardice in giving in to the authorities and asserts that his secret composition of the *Discorsi* is not a triumph but a defeat. Exactly what Brecht intended by this is by no means clear on the surface. It becomes somewhat clearer when we realize that Brecht never intended Galileo to be the true protagonist of the play: "The 'hero' of the work is . . . not Galilei but the people, as Walter Benjamin pointed out."[42] It is also necessary to realize that Brecht did not intend his intensely unfavorable portrait of the Roman Catholic church to refer to the church at all: it referred to authority per se—in modern times to political rather than ecclesiastical authority.[43] Galileo's final didactic speech to Andrea thus becomes a condemnation of scientists who give in to the pressures of "patriotism" as defined by the political authorities:

I take it the intent of science is to ease human existence. If you give way to coercion, science can be crippled, and your new machines may simply suggest new drudgeries. Should you then, in time, discover all there is to be discovered, your progress must then become a progress away from the bulk of humanity. The gulf might even grow so wide that the sound of your cheering at some new achievement would be echoed by a universal howl of horror. . . . I have come to believe that I was never in real danger; for some years I was as strong as the authorities, and I surrendered my knowledge to the powers that be, to use it, no, not *use* it, *abuse* it, as it suits their ends. I have betrayed my profession. Any man who does what I have done must not be tolerated in the ranks of science.[44]

The speech is an extremely forceful one, but the audience would have to perform some exceedingly convoluted intellectual gymnastics to get Brecht's point. It is not instantly obvious to the average spectator that Pope Urban, Cardinal Bellarmin, and the Cardinal Inquisitor represent not the church but political authority and that Galileo's cowardice on being shown the instruments of torture is analogous to the capitulation of modern scientists in the face of political pressure. Most of them, after all, capitulated eagerly, and not at all because they feared the consequences of defiance. In hindsight Galileo—or any modern scientist who feels pangs of guilt at having handed the fruits of his disinterested experimentation to the political authorities—may have felt that he could have defied the authorities with impunity; but at the time neither Galileo nor any other scientist could have known that. And impunity is certainly not one of the attributes of the scientist in the modern totalitarian state. There is a far more accurate animadversion on the condition of the scientist—or, indeed, any thinker—in the totalitarian state in two lines in the fourth scene where Galileo is vainly trying to persuade the philosophers and mathematicians at the Florentine court to look through his telescope at the Jovian moons:

GALILEO: Are we, as scholars, concerned with where the truth might lead us?

PHILOSOPHER: Mr. Galilei, the truth might lead us anywhere![45]

In the first, preatomic, version the Philosopher's reply is
fatuously comic; in the second it becomes ominous and sinister. The lines do not change, but their meaning has changed
because the context of the audience's thought has changed.
The continuing suitability of a play's message to the changing
context of the audience's thought is, of course, the key to a
play's survival; and it is because of the relevance of the message
of *Galileo* that the play will continue to survive, as will *Mother
Courage, The Good Woman of Sezuan*, and *The Caucasian Chalk
Circle*. The fact that Brecht did not intend Mother Courage,
Shen-Te, Grusha, or Galileo to represent individual human
indomitability in the face of overwhelming adversity is irrelevant. It is the philosophical context of an age—as filtered
down from the intelligentsia to the general public in the form
of attitudes and poses—that determines a play's meaning and
its reception as well. Brecht's exile dramas are a perfect example of the fact that an author may be habitually magical in his
thinking and yet—to the benefit, at least, of his reputation in a
democratic society—be interpreted analytically.

Brecht's work is a paradigm for the analytic drama, its failure and its triumph, for it provides the clue that gives us the
reason for the split we have seen between true analytic drama
and what I have called magical drama. Analytic drama is
founded on a philosophy that expresses—ever so cautiously,
ever so tentatively—a faith in the ability of the human being to
better himself by his own efforts and to achieve a sense of his
own integrity from within himself. In analytic drama the human being is portrayed as having choices and controlling his
own fate within the context of his temporal life and of the social
milieu that has partially—and *only* partially!—shaped it. Like
Ibsen's protagonists, Grusha, the servant girl in *The Caucasian
Chalk Circle*, makes the moral decisions that determine her life.
Shen-Te, too, makes her decisions, though the society in which
she lives restricts their scope. Galileo and Mother Courage, like
Mrs. Alving, fail to make decisions at crucial moments in their

lives, and thus fall victim to a social determinism whose fragility they fail to comprehend. In the *Lehrstücke*, however, Brecht shows his characters as ciphers, just as Shaw in his later drama showed them as embodied philosophical attitudes. This depersonalization of the characters in favor of an abstract thematic schematism is typical of magical drama, as the leap to an apocalyptic synthesis, either through the omission of the antithesis or by the use of a synthesis that does not follow in a direct logical sequence from the propositions, is its keynote. The playwright who has abandoned analytic drama for magical drama imagines the existence of a state of affairs that seems to him desirable and uses his characters like pieces in a chess game that has only pawns on the board. In other words, the writer plays God. That is the key to the distinction: Magical drama represents a resurgence of the religious attitude abandoned by both fragmentational and analytic drama. For Brecht that resurgence involved his submersion in the dogmatics of Communism, which, with its wish-fulfillment fantasy of a classless light illuminating a New Jerusalem of industrial bliss at the end of the capitalistic tunnel, is just as much a religion as any of the supernatural systems. For Shaw it involved the invention of a personal, purely earthbound religion based on a genetic fantasy of progressive mutations of Man to Superman through the agency of an undefined and undefinable but nevertheless blandly apotheosized Life Force.

The advent of magical drama did not spell the end of analytic drama. The hard logic of existentialist philosophy revived the confidence in the human being's control over his fate that was Ibsen's principal thesis, although it did so only in isolated instances. The best recent example that we have of analytic drama is Jean-Paul Sartre's *The Flies*. In this remarkable modernization of the *Oresteia* Sartre gives the clearest exposition of existentialist philosophy and thereby of analytic drama, which is always intellectually based on existential thought. Whereas Aeschylus wrote what was essentially a didactic patriotic tract intended to indoctrinate the audience in the sanctity of the Athenian law, Sartre has written an affirmation of the powerlessness of superimposed law.

Sartre's protagonists are Zeus and Orestes. The latter has returned to Argos, just as in the ancient version, but not for revenge. He has returned merely out of curiosity and feels himself completely detached from the events that have taken place there. After his meeting with Electra he changes his mind and kills Aegistheus and Clytemnestra. The difficulty in understanding Sartre's play lies in the character of Zeus. In the text of the play Zeus is portrayed as being in the guise of an ordinary traveler like Orestes who does everything he can to persuade the latter to leave Argos without revenging himself. Much more important, however, he is subtextually the personification of the idea of religion. Since religion does not exist in Sartre's intellectual system, Zeus does not exist in reality either but appears real in the play because he is the embodied belief in himself. God, in other words, is given substance by being imagined but becomes powerless and nonexistent the moment belief is withdrawn—an elegant modern refutation of Anselmic ontology. For fifteen years, ever since the murder of Agamemnon, Argos has been repenting. It is a city obsessed with guilt and thus completely under the domination of religious belief. Zeus, who embodies the idea of religion, and Aegistheus, who embodies the political power that is always shored up by the invented supernatural political system that we call religion, want to keep it that way. Aegistheus believes himself secure, but Zeus knows better, just as the archbishops who conferred the "divine" right to wield absolute power on kings and emperors by crowning them before the high altar knew better. Aegistheus believes that he is just the shadow of Zeus, who is in platonic terms the idea of man, the ultimate reality. But Zeus knows that he cannot even cast a shadow: he is only an abstract artefact spuriously representing an invented system. "You and I," Zeus explains to Aegistheus, "harbor the same dark secret in our hearts."[46] Aegistheus protests that he has no secret, but Zeus reveals it to him. It is "The bane of gods and kings. The bitterness of knowing men are free. Yes, Aegistheus, they are free. But your subjects do not know it, and you do." Aegistheus realizes the truth: "A free man in a city acts like a plague-spot." A free man is no more acceptable than an upright man was in Sodom or Gomorrah. "Once freedom lights its beacon in a man's heart," Zeus laments, "the gods are powerless against him."

Once Orestes has decided to take action—has made his own unaided decision—and avenged his father by killing Aegistheus and his mother, he realizes he is free. Free and utterly alone, for it is no relief to be released from the comforts of bondage. Once Orestes is free he is "beyond remedy, except what remedy I find within myself. . . . I am doomed to have no other law but mine" (act 3). Electra, horrified by the act she desired so much and urged Orestes to commit, repents and succumbs to the Flies, Sartre's version of the Eumenides. Orestes, however, is immune and walks through them untouched, for he simply does not believe in them. Zeus reproaches Orestes for having done the people great harm by showing them the truth, but Orestes answers him in a magnificent passage that sums up the essence of existentialist thought and the analytic attitude toward life:

> ZEUS: . . . You will tear from their eyes the veils I had laid on them, and they will see their lives as they are, foul and futile, a barren boon.
> ORESTES: Why, since it is their lot, should I deny them the despair I have in me?
> ZEUS: What will they make of it?
> ORESTES: What they choose. They're free; and human life begins on the far side of despair.
>
> (Act 3)

"Human life begins on the far side of despair." It is a hard lesson, one that Camus was to develop in *The Myth of Sisyphus* and in *The Rebel,* where he asserts that man triumphs over his fate in direct proportion to his defiance of it and his stubborn insistence on defining his own. The paradox of the analytic drama is that the self can define its own reality only through the realization and acceptance of despair as its lot. To pass through despair is to pass through to freedom, which is the acceptance of solitude and total self-responsibility.

Unfortunately, true analytic drama like *The Flies* is morally too rigorous and intellectually too harsh for most people. The comforting message of magical drama seduces even the intellectuals, who should know better. In philosophy, as in life, the psychological evasion of thinking in terms of "if only . . ." is almost universally prevalent. It is not, unhappily, the astringent clear-sightedness of a Sartre that is accepted, however unwillingly, by contemporary intellectual thought but rather the detached urbanity of a quintessentially magical dramatist like the Giraudoux of *The Madwoman of Chaillot.* Most typical magical dramas project the desired state far into the future, like all true religious works. Giraudoux offers instant satisfaction. That what he offers is a fantasized satisfaction does not make it any the less satisfying. The fantasy makes it less sensible, but it makes it more theatrical. The quintessential magical drama restores to the theater its status as an escapist world of illusions of which it had been robbed by the advent of modern thought, of fragmentational and analytic thought, brought about by the loss of faith in religion. For religion is no more than theater raised to the nth degree.

CHAPTER 3

Synthesis

The breakdown of belief that resulted in fragmentational and analytic thinking could not last. Fragmentational thought was an emotional reaction to the social trauma that produced it, and it carried the seeds of its own destruction within it from its very beginning. The fragmentational mode of thought is the mayfly of philosophy. Whenever it springs up—and it does so periodically, for the ecstatic outburst of despair is triggered ever anew—it does so explosively and then subsides again. Its most extreme form, Dada, explicitly made its self-destruction part of its program; but the image of disintegration could not be sustained indefinitely in any case. Analytic thought had no such problems. Where Jarry has Ubu say that even the ruins must be razed to the ground, the analytic thinkers concentrated only on building up. They were optimists who envisioned a new era in which the mistakes of the past would be buried beneath the gleaming, streamlined structures of the future. The theory was impeccable; but it foundered on the reefs of reality. The analytic playwrights painfully rediscovered an old truth: men could not be cajoled into changing; they could only be forced. And so they turned to magical drama, building up magnificent vistas of perfect worlds peopled by Supermen, devoid of class distinctions, and without evil. Analytic drama had turned in desperation to fantasy and had become social science fiction. The only playwright who perceived the true nature of analytic thought after Ibsen was Jean-Paul Sartre. Like Ibsen, he saw that the freedom men realized they had after their liberation from the bondage of religious thought had to be attained individually. Improvement could come about only through the fortuitous collective force of many individual wills, but never through the attempted imposition of a social plan. Man, as Sartre demonstrates in *The Flies,* is completely and absolutely free within himself, not subject even to hereditary influences. Sartrian free man is embodied in Orestes. His triumph over the Flies and over Zeus represents Sartre's assertion that freedom is possible, but it leaves us wondering whether it is not an idealized concept. Something that is as rare as triumphant self-willed and self-created freedom tends to be covered with an aura of unreality. Orestes embodies a philosophy, but he is not convincing as a person. A more realistic view of the extreme individualist is to be found in the person of Möbius in Dürrenmatt's *The Physicists.* Like Orestes, Möbius creates his own fate and asserts his own freedom, but with his typical sardonic view of life Dürrenmatt has him decide that freedom is possible only in imprisonment; and then discover that even there it is not possible.

Möbius is the ultimate analytical man, and he fails. *The Physicists* is the play that marks the transition from analytic and magical thinking to synthetic thinking. Plays imbued with the synthetic mode of thought had been written before *The Physi-*

cists, of course, but Dürrenmatt's play marked the change and defined its nature.

The Physicists takes place in a lunatic asylum, the appropriate place from Dürrenmatt's point of view for the fate of the world to be worked out. Three physicists are confined here under the care of a grotesque, humpbacked female psychiatrist. One of the physicists insists that he is really Sir Isaac Newton and appears in seventeenth-century dress and wig. Another insists that he is Einstein, appears in appropriate makeup, and saws away at his violin to calm his nerves. The third, Möbius, proclaims that King Solomon appears to him in visions. Möbius has been shut up for fifteen years; the others are recent arrivals. All three, it turns out, are perfectly sane. Newton and Einstein, besides being eminent physicists, are agents of the secret services of capitalistic and Communist powers, respectively, each sent to persuade Möbius to come back with him. Möbius is a myth figure. He is, as Newton puts it, the greatest physicist—indeed, the greatest brain—of all time. In Möbius is the culmination of all human intellectual striving. He is the embodiment of ultimate human achievement. Möbius has solved the problem of gravity and discovered the unified field theory of the elements, and worked out the system of all possible discoveries. In short, he has the power not only to explicate the nature of the universe but to master the world through the system of all possible discoveries, which he says he elaborated out of sheer curiosity as a practical addendum to his theoretical work. Möbius has deliberately faked madness and has voluntarily condemned himself to perpetual imprisonment in the lunatic asylum in order to prevent his discoveries from falling into the wrong hands. He feels that humanity is not yet ready—perhaps never will be—to be given the knowledge that he has uncovered, that it would only use that knowledge for partisan destructive purposes. He feels that the scientist has a moral duty to consider the effects of his discoveries and to sacrifice his own ambition and potential fame for the common good. Technological progress has far outstripped moral sense, he feels, and, with Dürrenmatt's typically sardonic reversal of values, he explicates the paradox of freedom in the modern world to his two fellow scientists: "We can still be free only in a lunatic asylum. Only there can we still think. Out there our thoughts are dynamite. . . . Either we remain in the madhouse or the world will become one. Either we snuff ourselves out from the minds of mankind or mankind itself will be snuffed out. . . . We are wild beasts. We must not be let loose upon mankind."[1] In a magnificent passage that might be termed the last stand of analytic theater he persuades the other two to give up their careers and their freedom forever: "Insane but wise. Imprisoned but free. Physicists but guiltless."[2] Their perverse, self-sacrificing triumph is short-lived, however. As Möbius himself says when he realizes the truth, "What has once been thought can never be unthought again."[3] Möbius' papers have been secretly photocopied by Dr. von Zahnd, the grotesque psychiatrist, who really is insane and really believes that King Solomon appears to her. With Möbius' all-encompassing formula she has taken over the world and made all mankind her slaves. While Möbius has been amusing himself with his calculations and preening himself on his moral stance, she has acted and has robotized humanity in her service. The misshapen harpy, sterile in her virginity—a state she insistently proclaims— has succeeded in twisting the world into her own image, the image of something no longer quite human and not yet quite machine. If knowledge is power, she is omnipotent; and omnipotence is an attribute of divinity. This human being that is already more than half machine has resuscitated the concept of God—an inhuman God of cams and ratchets to replace the superhuman God of thunderbolts and political pronunciamentos.

Dürrenmatt's *The Physicists* is one of the pivotal plays of the modern drama, a play that marks the transition from one mode of thought to another. It is not a pioneering play like Jarry's, which appeared on the scene with no antecedents in the previous drama, but it defined, rather, a change that had been taking place gradually but had not yet been fully accepted. After *The Physicists* the recognition of that change could no longer be avoided. What had happened was that the two philosophical reactions to the elimination of the metaphysical dimension brought on by the shock waves of the scientific and French revolutions had been found wanting. Their inadequacy had nothing to do with any demonstration of their lack of validity. No such demonstration has ever been made. They had been found wanting because they gave no emotional satisfaction. Mankind continues to crave the assurance of a greater power; and so, after a lapse of millennia, a greater power had to be invented again. This time, however, since, as Möbius points out, "What has once been thought can never be unthought again," it had to be a purely physical and thus *admittedly* man-made power. Man could no longer postulate an invisible God, creating and yet inexplicably eternal and uncreated, but had to create an extension of himself to bow down to.

It is here that we come to the third main philosophical stream of modern drama: the synthetic drama. Synthetic drama is a metaphor of the transformation of man into machine through the mechanization of the social structure—and, consequently, of its parts. It is simultaneously a culmination and a regression. It draws together the disillusionment and the despair of the two earlier trends into an amalgamation that is neither despair nor hope, but a recognition of a world that has changed. At the same time it is also a reversion to a premodern view of the world in which the individual was secondary to a greater power. That power is the machine. Man has created his own deity once again, but this time it is a concretely tangible one based on his own technological discoveries rather than a vaporously intangible one based on the political speculations of a few. The mist-wreathed pythoness of the oracle had been replaced by the spinning tape decks of the computer.

The synthetic drama, properly speaking, has its immediate philosophical underpinnings in the science of cybernetics, which defines the theory whereby the man-made machine masters its creator. But, like all philosophical movements, it had its prophets. The synthetic drama had its beginnings in that extraordinary and anachronistic work, Georg Büchner's *Woyzeck*. *Woyzeck* is a play that, although written in 1836, is only just now coming into its own. Indeed, in many respects it still seems an avant-garde play since the full impact of its meaning was literally unintelligible for so long. *Woyzeck* is, in fact, a precursor of both the synthetic and the absurd drama. The absurd element is not really an integral part of the play and occurs solely in the Grandmother's scene, which seems to be inserted purely for the purpose of expressing Büchner's eschatological world view since it has no relation to the action of the play at all. Nevertheless, its foreshadowing of the path one aspect of fragmentational philosophy was to take is so extraordinary that it is as perfect an imaginative summation of absurdism as we have. The contrast between the setting of a group of little girls begging the Grandmother to tell them a story and the content of the diabolically warped fairy tale that she responds with is in itself horrifying enough, but the story is worth quoting for its own sake:

> Once upon a time there was a poor child that had no father or mother because everyone was dead and there wasn't anyone on the earth anymore. Everyone was dead and so it went and looked night and day. And because there wasn't anyone on the earth anymore it wanted to go to heaven, and the moon looked at it in such a nice way. But when it finally got to the moon it found that the moon was just a piece of rotten wood. And so it went to the sun, but when it came to the sun it found that the sun was just a faded sunflower. And when it came to the stars it found that the stars were like little golden bugs stuck on thorns by a shrike. And when it wanted to get back to the earth, it found that the earth was a broken pot. And so it was all alone. And so it sat down and cried, and it's still sitting there and is still all alone.[4]

Only Beckett has managed to give us a comparable metaphoric picture of man's suspension in an impersonal (and therefore unrelievedly cruel) void.

The principal thrust of *Woyzeck* is social and psychological rather than metaphysical, however. Büchner was the first playwright to perceive that society is a machine. Who designed the machine remains a mystery. Most probably it evolved itself, that is to say, the components of the social hierarchy unconsciously subjugated themselves to the rules they had developed. The rules became immutable abstractions that stripped the individual will of all power and turned men imperceptibly into robots. All the characters in the play except Woyzeck are such automated creatures. Woyzeck's tragedy is that he has faint glimmerings in his mind of the senselessness and injustice of this system that is based on a universal "debraining" machine, to use Ubu's phrase, set up by mankind to operate on its creators. The social machine, as Büchner sees it, is a means of replacing mental activity and thus consciousness of self. The slightest sign of such consciousness breaks the mold and renders the possessor unfit for further participation in the robotized society. To become human, as Woyzeck begins to do, is an act that condemns him to destruction. In the world that Büchner foresaw, survival is paradoxically possible only through dehumanization. The choice is between death and death-in-life. The latter state is lived in, obviously, by Andres, Woyzeck's friend. Andres is the image of what Woyzeck *should* be, what he has been designed to become: an id controlled by the collective superego that is society. All the other principal characters of the play, the Captain, the Doctor, Marie, the Drum Major are versions of Andres, each performing his coglike task from a different perch on the social pyramid. The acquiescence to enslavement by a collective version of themselves which these characters display is the result of their allowing their existence to be defined by essences imposed on them from outside instead of formulated by themselves. This *may* be due to genetic debility, as it seems to be in the case of Andres, or it may be the result of failure to develop a personal ego, thus exposing the primal existential id to the control of a superego. A superego in this sense is an ego that feels insufficient unto itself and turns outward to impose itself on others in an attempt to assure itself of its own validity and rectitude. The Doctor and the Captain display this in their attitudes to Woyzeck, but they are merely faint reflections of the massive collective uncertainty that drives the social machine of which they are all unconscious parts. Tyranny such as the Captain and the Doctor practice on Woyzeck is an expression of the tyrant's frustration at his own impotence. Each level of society attempts to enslave the level below in an instinctive reaction against the tacit knowledge of its own enslavement. Woyzeck shows the first faint gropings of rebellion against this system. As soon as he does so, he is marked for destruction. In writing *Woyzeck* Büchner showed the fatal effects of rebelling against the megamachine of society and pointed the way to a theme that was to become important in drama only one hundred or more years later.

Büchner, writing during the Industrial Revolution, saw that society was transforming itself into a machine and using its human components as parts of the machine. The social machine that he foresaw might be imagined as an enormous pyramidal bank of pigeonholes from each of which a human being pops out on demand like the cuckoo in a cuckoo clock to perform his special function. The inexorable advance of technology would gradually metamorphose this structure into an organic computerized data bank. The social megamachine uses its makers as its parts; it is a creation that incorporates its creators. It is a macrocosmic biofeedback machine linked in a perverse organic relationship with its parts, controlling them yet controlled by them. It is the new secular deity, and the cybernetic engineers are its priests and acolytes. The hollowness of the concept of the traditional God had left an intolerable void in the minds of men. That void had to be filled. No longer subjected to the abstract, men had to subject themselves to the concrete. The traditional God, who had been killed off philosophically by his forcible severance from the body politic (the real source of his power) by the French Revolution, had been the invention of the Intangible and Invisible in order to explain the tangible and visible. The suprahuman machine that replaced him is the invention of the tangible and visible in order to block out the fear of the assumed presence of something intangible and invisible that pervades the inexplicable void beyond the bounds of consciously perceived existence.

The new God is worshiped under several forms, although, in contrast to the old God, it is depersonalized and is always worshiped unconsciously. The old God continues, of course, as a consciously worshiped entity, personalized in the minds of most people as an omnipotent patriarchal figure. For most people, however, only the ritual of religion survives while its underlying myths have degenerated into fairy tales. In modern times new myths have sprung up: the myth of the all-enveloping social megamachine and the myth of the Utopia to be created by the "system of all possible discoveries." The first myth has replaced the religious moral code, the second embodies the hopes formerly placed in the Second Coming. The new religion has its rites as well, one of which is the systematic corruption of language. The slogan has replaced prayer. While prayer may have been senseless, objectively speaking, since it was a supplication of the void, it was at least a direct and specific supplication. The slogan, on the other hand, may be defined as a phrase that reassures and inspires through the removal of meaning. Man becomes united to the collective human machine through the ritualistic utterance of catchword phrases that have a soothing subjective meaning while relentlessly destroying objective meaning—or, in other words, the possibility of the perception of reality.

The corruption of language by language, whether through slogans or by other means, is a process usually associated in modern times with totalitarian regimes. Indeed, totalitarian regimes are arguably based primarily on the manipulation of language: we have become too "civilized" to look upon arms as a self-justifying end in themselves. In the past "the will of God" as interpreted by those privy to its enigmatic undulations of purpose was sufficient justification for the exercise of power; but since the dissolution of that concept more elaborate linguistic contortions have come to be deemed necessary. Totalitarianism is the conception of man and society as a machine and of language as an instrument for programming it. It is, thus, not surprising that playwrights living under totalitarian regimes are the foremost practitioners of synthetic drama, for they are inevitably more perceptive of and sensitive to the structure of the machine that engulfs them. In a "free" society that structure is masked, and its components are frequently unaware of the role they are playing. A "free" society is one in which the charade of free will is played out on a deterministic set; in a totalitarian society the skeletal structure of the set is visible to the actors.

A good example of an unintentionally synthetic drama in a "free" society is Arthur Miller's *Death of a Salesman*. Miller's intention was clearly twofold: to write an analytic drama posing the problem of the ordinary worker in a conscienceless, capitalistic society and implicitly condemning the system; and to write a modern tragedy adapting Aristotelian theory to allow for a common man as tragic protagonist. Miller's success in achieving his stated aims has been the subject of considerable debate, principally among those critics who feel that an adherence to Aristotelian guidelines for the writing of tragedy is still important. Miller himself has argued that tragedy consists of "the underlying fear of being displaced, the disaster inherent in being torn away from our chosen image of what and who we are in the world."[5] As a definition of tragedy this is perhaps as valid as any, but it does not apply to Miller's protagonist. Willy Loman is indeed torn away from his image of what and who he is in the world, but that image was never chosen by him. Willy is under the delusion that he has chosen his self-image, but it has in fact been chosen for him, as it has been for the millions who make up the common horde that Miller intends Willy to represent. It is here that the feedback mechanism of the sociohuman machine becomes evident. The common man has not chosen his self-image, nor has it been deliberately devised by some powerful individual Machiavellian mind and artfully insinuated to him as his own. The common man's relation to the social machine is a symbiotic one, and the creation of his image of himself is accomplished reciprocally between himself and the multiplication of himself that constitutes the major part of society. It is based simultaneously on the need of the mass to cohere and form the mortar that holds itself together and the individual's need to belong to something other than himself—in short, to bow down to something greater than himself. Willy Loman and those he represents are the victims of a delusion collectively created by themselves and believed in and worshiped as fervently as any deity ever was. Willy's mind is incapable of independent thought and therefore of self-realization. It is a befuddled mess of slogans derived from the flimflam of advertising jargon and the cant of popularized palliative psychology. And he uses these stock phrases as verbal talismans to ward off reality and self-realization, much as the invocation of imagined creatures in another world was once believed effective in warding off the imagined evil of this one.

Willy Loman is the compleat synthetic man as well as the prototypical common man Miller intends him to be. Willy *believes.* He believes in the myths of the capitalistic society in which he is subsumed. He believes in the myth of log cabin to president, which he transforms into a myth of seedy drudge to big business executive. He believes in the pot of gold at the end of the rainbow, realized in his mind by his brother Ben who walked into the jungle and came out rich. He believes in appearance, in phoniness, in acceptance ("not just liked, but well liked") by those he regards as the gods of the machine. Above all, he believes in advertising slogans: "Chevrolet, Linda, is the greatest car ever built." But somehow his faith does not sustain him ("That goddam Chevrolet, they ought to prohibit the manufacture of that car"), and he has to work harder and harder, bolster his self-delusion more and more to sustain his feeling of integration. At the end he is spewed out by the machine as a useless part and desperately immolates himself in his faith by dying so his son can collect the insurance money and thus pay his entrance fee at the portals of the machine he had left to seek the hard reality of self-realization.

Willy lives and moves around in the seedy precincts of lower-middle-class New York City and in the salesman's northeast territory, venturing occasionally and always abortively into the head offices of the Company at the center of the city. Practiced eyes will have no difficulty in recognizing this setting as a concrete version of the abstract and symbolic village at the base of Kafka's *Castle* where K. meets much the same fate as Willy. Just as Dürrenmatt's *The Physicists* is the definitive statement of the futility of analytic drama with its creation and destruction of Möbius, the ultimate analytic thinker, and his useless artificial melioristic morality, so Kafka's Castle is the paradigmatic symbol of the world that is the setting in various guises of the synthetic drama. Just as Möbius is the ultimate analytic man, so K. is the ultimate synthetic man. He comes to the village desperately wishing to be swallowed up in it and spends his life seeking to make obeisance, to lose whatever latent possibility for individuality he may have. The village, grasped in the invisible tentacles of the Castle, seems to exist in the void. The Castle itself differs from the village only in being high above it, both physically and hierarchically. It is not, in fact, a castle at all but apparently another village. It is, in other words, the machine that controls society, but it is only a more elaborate replica of that society, staffed by functionaries who are merely larger cogs than the villagers. Computers are capable of themselves creating more elaborate computers that are capable of programming their creators; and the Castle is the creation of the village, but the memory of the act has been lost in the succession of generations. The process is analogous to the genesis of traditional religion. Man creates God and then subjugates himself to his own creation and to the functionaries who have taken over its operation.

Art is not a statement of fact, nor is it a representation of reality: it is criticism. Art is reality transformed. Analytic art is reality improved; fragmentational art is reality distorted and nullified; synthetic art is a satiric depiction of mechanized reality. Synthetic art shows man with the human element excised. To show man as machine is to write science fiction. Synthetic art, like all art, criticizes: it shows the inadequacy of the machine and satirizes man's continued blind dependence on the false god he has created. Kafka's Castle does not work. The offices are filled with columns of documents that constantly crash to the ground in billows of dust. The phones are not connected to a central switchboard, are usually left off the hook, and are answered, when they are answered at all, with random frivolousness by minor officials who invariably know nothing of the caller's affairs. Although the omnipotence and omniscience of the Castle officials are passionately—perhaps desperately—believed in by the masses in the village, no one in the Castle really knows what he is doing or what the higher purposes of his actions are. Everything is done in accordance with meaningless and desiccated rules and regulations that seem never to have had any meaning in the first place. Each official believes that he is doing his part in carrying out the inscrutable but actually never expressed edicts that supposedly emanate from the vacuous Holy of Holies at the undiscoverable center of the Castle. The credulously worshiped machine constantly malfunctions and breaks down, buried under the suffocating detritus of its overloaded memory bank.

Kafka's art grew out of his nightmarish visions. When he died in 1924 those visions had not yet become actuality. They were soon to do so. The rise of the modern totalitarian state; the discovery of the principles of cybernetics, which revealed the analogy between man and machine and paved the way for research into the manipulation of the human brain; and the monstrous complexity and impersonality of the sociopolitical structure in even comparatively free nations all contributed to the actualization of Kafka's fantasy. It has increasingly become the function of dramatic art to reflect and criticize this state of affairs, well described by the distinguished Catalan critic Xavier Fàbregas as "the feeling of helplessness in the face of a society ever more technologically controlled, where the act of decision which has up to now been the province of the human being has fallen into the hands of a complex and acephalous organism—or, simply, into the hands of electronic devices."[6]

The feeling of being a helpless pawn in the hands of forces outside oneself, whether electronic or otherwise, is nowhere so intense as in an absolute totalitarian society. Usually in such a society theatrical activity is confined to propagandistic claptrap or innocuous escape plays. The Spanish and Catalan drama under Franco was a notable exception, and, although written without hope of production in its own society, provides a rich body of literature in the synthetic mode. The Catalan novelist and playwright Manuel de Pedrolo, an enormously prolific writer who, were he writing in one of the major languages, would be world renowned, has been particularly adept at creating dramatic metaphors for a mechanized society in which people worship their own collectively created fossilized and ineffable system. *L'ús de la matèria* (The Use of Matter, 1963) has been aptly described as a picture of what Kafka's Castle might look like on the inside.[7] The play takes place in an obscure and dusty cubbyhole of an office—windowless, of course—tucked away in the labyrinthine passageways of the social megamachine. The office is full of moldering files, and the two clerks who occupy it do nothing but sign papers. They do not read them; they merely sign them. They are cogs in the machine and know nothing of what goes on beyond the surrounding cogs. Their only emotions are fear of their superiors and resentment of those who are still outside the machine or organization or system of which they have become a part—who "do things" and "live," as one of them puts it. To remedy this situation and provide more employment inside the machine, one of them comes up with a plan to divide the task of signing documents so that there will be specialists in writing each letter and in dotting the *i*'s, and crossing the *t*'s, and inserting the periods. We get the other side of this picture in Kafka, where the villagers are desperately and suicidally trying to become part of the staff of the Castle. At another point in the play the two clerks are ordered to destroy all the incomplete files in the office, which is the same as saying all the files, in order to eliminate "everything superfluous and a good deal of what is necessary." They are, however, cautioned in the next breath to keep three copies of each paper they destroy. The two clerks have neither family nor private lives, like the officials in the Castle, and during the course of the action they kill two intruders who threaten to upset the routine by which they exist. In both cases the killings are done absolutely impersonally, without emotion or consciousness of moral aberration, the "crime" of the victims being disregard of the regulations of the organization.

The criticism that is art shows itself in the demonstration of the moral and operational chaos inside the megamachine. This point is made over and over in the synthetic drama. The machine runs the world we know, and it does not work. The closer one approaches the vacuous Holy of Holies, the pre-cariously balanced seat of power in political terms, the less one's connection with the rest of the human race. Absorption by the machine turns human beings into ciphers, so that we are finally faced with a vision of a world guided by robots. But here too Lord Acton's maxim holds true: absolute power corrupts absolutely even when the holders are no longer human. The universality of Lord Acton's observation is, indeed, based on the fact that the possession and exercise of power separate the holder from the safeguards necessarily inherent in contact with other people. With the accession of power the holder is cast loose in a morally valueless void, like Camus' Caligula.

Manuel de Pedrolo also shows his vision of life outside the precincts of the Castle/megamachine. Both *Situació bis* (Full Circle, 1958) and *Cruma* (1957) are versions of life in the village below, though they show different aspects of it. *Situació bis* is more directly pertinent to Kafka's vision. Like Kafka, Pedrolo sees human beings as controlled by inscrutable and ultimately senseless decrees that come from some superior and blindly obeyed but still human power. His dramatic metaphor takes us to an enclosed space inhabited by four males and four females. Each one lives alone in one of the numbered rooms that surround a central open space. Their sterile and impersonal existences are completely focused on a large wastepaper basket in the center of the open space. Several times a day two men from the outside, one carrying a stick, the other a sack, come in and empty a pile of letters into the basket. The inhabitants fall on the letters, which are not addressed to them and never contain anything of interest to them, like famished beasts on food and carry them into their rooms, where they devour them in the ever vain hope of some day finding something of use to them in the writings. The laws by which they live and which they obey unquestioningly require them to be in their rooms when the mail is delivered. Anyone caught outside his room may be killed by the man with the stick. The latter violates the law by chasing one of the inhabitants into her room and killing her there, and the others thereupon decide to take the law into their own hands and change it. When they next appear with the letters the two men from outside are killed and replaced by the ringleader of the revolt and one other elected by the rest. On their first return after being appointed letter carriers the two are transformed into instruments of the higher power and give no other explanation than the superiority of those outside who make the laws. When their former friends rebel and refuse to accept their authority, they kill them one by one. As soon as they step outside they become absorbed into the senseless machinery of the Castle and turn into the oppressors of their (former) fellow beings. The important thing to notice here is that Pedrolo, like Kafka, is creating an overall metaphor for the condition of the human being as a living part of the social machine.

Pedrolo creates a similar metaphor in *Homes i No* (Men and No, 1957). Here two families live and grow old in two cages separated by a narrow corridor occupied by their jailer, No, a symbol of the negation of the human right of self-determination in life. At the end they manage to overcome No, but their hopes of leaving their cages are dashed by the revelation that an apparently infinite series of cages stretches beyond them, and that their jailer is imprisoned in the corridor between their cages. They fight for freedom only to find that it is unattainable because they are part of an infinitely elaborate system of entrapment in which the guardians are themselves guarded. The only possible response to a perception of such a situation is submission and acceptance, which is tantamount to worship. The difference is that neither No nor his avatars, neither the cages on the stage nor their endless multiplications beyond, are transcendent. They are the visible and tangible signs of a strictly earthbound and man-made system: the totalitarian state raised to the status of a latter-day City of God.

The attempt to break out of the cage is futile, as the two families in Pedrolo's *Homes i No* demonstrate. Nor is there any hope in the younger generation since their more determined rebellion against the system only serves to show them that the system is indestructible, that man has constructed a prison around himself and tossed away the key. Or, to put it another way, he has built a machine, programmed it to rule him by taking care of all his material needs, and forgotten how to control it. He can neither reprogram it nor pull the plug and must submit to its rule instead. The result is shown in another Pedrolo play, *Cruma*. Modern man, as Cassirer has said, "can easily be thrown back into a state of complete acquiescence. He no longer questions his environment; he accepts it as a matter of course."[8] In *Cruma* we see the "new man"—totally programmed, totally acquiescent, cowering inside his cage and afraid to go out. The scene is a bare room with blank, white walls. The man who lives there, the Resident, has only a chair and an ashtray. He is visited, every day, by a friend, the Visitor. Every day, these two do something different to distract themselves and keep out the memory of the past, the threat of the present, and the dread of the future. This time when the Visitor enters, he finds the Resident measuring the walls. This is the "game for today"—the thing that they must do to keep out thought. This obsession of theirs is rather reminiscent of the "old jokes" in *Endgame* and *Waiting for Godot*. The game the two men play turns out to be a dud, for they find that the numbers have disappeared from their tape measures, which are now completely blank. They cannot measure the room anymore, which is tantamount to saying that they cannot make sense of their world. The world, perhaps, did make sense once when it was simpler and the products of technology had not yet encroached on human life so completely. "Cruma" is the name of an Etruscan unit of measurement, which, like everything else from that culture, is lost to us. The world that the Etruscans knew could, possibly, have been measured and understood by them, but the world as it is today cannot be measured and understood by us. Another aspect of the play is the Resident's inability to relate to other people. His world is enclosed by the walls of his room. He is, as it were, a monad floating through existence unaware of the other particles he meets. People pass through his room to an inner room, where, he tells his friend, all are dead, but he cannot distinguish these people and insists they are "nobody." When the Visitor goes to the bathroom, a completely different man, the Stranger, comes out, but nothing will convince the Resident that this is another person. If he did admit the difference he would have to relate to yet another person, and that would mean breaking his carefully constructed cocoon and letting chaos in. The Resident is at the bottom of the social pyramid. He does not even worship the self-deified mass of which he constitutes an indistinguishable grain, as do the two functionaries in *L'ús de la matèria*. He has become totally deindividualized and as obsolete as the Etruscan measure from which the play takes its name.

The obsoleteness of the human being as an individual and his transformation into a machine part will occupy more and more dramatists. The popular dramatist reflects the mores of the moment, and his plays are as lasting as the ephemeral trends he reflects. The dramatist of ideas—the analytical dramatist, the fragmentational dramatist, and now the synthetic dramatist—both reflects and prophesies. He observes the trends of his times and engages in a dialectical struggle with them. There is thus a greater time lag in his production. Instead of reflecting the moment, he encapsulates and criticizes the times. It is for this reason that the serious synthetic drama is still in its infancy; and it is for this reason, also, that there is such a dearth of serious drama being written at the present time. We are in an interim period between the exhaustion of the absurd point of view (not because it has in any sense become invalidated but because of the limitation on its expression through dramatic metaphor) and the crystallization of the synthetic point of view. To the acceptance of that point of view as a reflection of an existing reality there is, naturally enough, a powerful psychological barrier since few will be willing to recognize the obsolescence of the individual and fewer still capable of fighting it.

It cannot be emphasized too strongly or too often that what distinguishes "modern times" from previous human history is the demise of religion. What died, however, was not religion per se but religion as it was traditionally known and practiced. Analysis and fragmentation were—and are—two intellectual attempts to cope with a godless world. Intellectual attempts, however, are effective only with intellectuals, and they are in a minority. The ordinary human being needs reassurance, he needs a sense of something greater than himself. Like any animal, he has a territorial instinct: he needs a designated place in the world and a justification of that place. In other words, he needs to have the incomprehensible made explicit, however improbably. As a result of the dissolution of the unified creed and its universally believed in suprahuman entity, man had to turn for his solutions and his reassurance to his more inventive fellow beings. The guru replaced God. In modern times the guru has assumed protean disguises. Man has placed his faith in the political Führer guru, the psychiatrist guru, and the preacher guru (who pretends to represent a higher power but is actually worshiped himself as the surrogate for the postulated power). This class includes the inventors of religions, the interpreters of exotic, usually Eastern, cults, and the Christian revivalist ranters. Those who still follow the traditional *forms* of religion do so out of a sense of habit and duty but place their real faith, often subconsciously, elsewhere. Usually they place it in the person of the political guru or, more and more frequently, in the person of that quintessentially modern prophet, the technologist guru. It is this latter that has created what we might call the Kafkaesque Castle structure of modern society. The essential difference between the new social order and the old is that the new one is impersonal. The individual is not a unit in it but part of the mass. It is the difference between an edifice built of a variety of variously shaped stones and one built of poured concrete. The old religion-based state had many totalitarian aspects, but it was based on a religion that placed the burden of personal moral responsibility squarely on each individual. Each person was thus the master of his own integrity and was *forced* to be a separate and unique individual because he believed in salvation and believed that his personal salvation depended on *him*. In the modern mechanized culture, on the other hand, men are taught to abrogate responsibility. The preacher guru promises salvation through ritualistic contortions or through a hypnotically induced feeling of rebirth; the political guru through total obedience and faith in him as the evident manifestation of the deity; the psychiatrist guru through an uncomplaining reconciliation to the social status quo by means of a nonviolent form of brainwashing; and finally the technologist guru through the metamorphosis of man into cipher, of individual uniqueness into a punched card which is then fed into the all-controlling machine like a sacrifice into the maw of Moloch.

Nigel Dennis' *Cards of Identity* is an illustration of the transformation of the human being by the psychiatrist guru. The play, adapted by the author from his earlier novel of the same name, deals with a group calling itself the Identity Club that specializes in the transformation of personalities. Their theory is based on the fact that man's grasp on his sense of identity is tenuous at best to begin with, and that the sense of self is based on one's wishful restructuring of one's memories. Man is not what he eats, in other words: man is what he remembers. By the subtle application of the power of suggestion man's memories of his own earlier experiences can be changed; and, therefore, he himself can be changed. Dennis shows this on an individual basis in the play, but, of course, the same principle applies to the mass. A people's cohesiveness, its sense of itself as a society or a nation, is based on its memory of its history. Here the task is much simpler, indeed. History is recorded, not individually experienced. Change the records, and the people's sense of itself and its mission or "manifest destiny" is changed also. The phenomenon has happened often enough, especially in modern times, when the techniques of mass propaganda have been refined and honed to a degree of perfection never before attained.

In the play itself five persons are transformed by having their memories of their own pasts restructured. Four of them are turned into servants at a country house which is to be used for a convention of the Identity Club. The fifth is turned into a murderer so that the president of the club can be disposed of and replaced by the protagonist. Dennis' perception of society's turn toward the synthetic structure can be seen in the introductory remarks he puts in the President's mouth at the opening of the convention:

> . . . For what *makes* the world in which we live today? Well: we hear much of something called "the individual." We hear

much of a body vaguely named "society." But what *are* these
. . . but ghosts—verbal vestiges, mere wisps of fantasy in the
brains of deluded librarians? The world of today is a world of
groups—of hard, fanatical groups of men, too united in their
aims for any one member to be individual . . . modern man is
accused repeatedly of having lost his religious sense—but, in
fact, has this world ever seen such an age of faith? What are
the miracles of the old religion, what are loaves, fishes and
risen Lazaruses, compared with the miracles of the cosmic
box, the libidinous couch, the charts, graphs and compost
heaps which are modern godheads? . . . There is no sort of
identity we are not able to create, no self so nonsensical that
we cannot make it plausible. We can make an average man
out of a Teddy Boy, a St. Augustine out of a Logical Positiv-
ist, a charitable man out of an Archbishop of Canterbury.

The individual is a ghost—a verbal vestige. Only the group
exists, and these groups constitute religions more powerful
even than the old religions they have replaced. The Identity
Club itself is simply another such religion, as completely convinced of its own exclusive rectitude as any other religion: "*We
know*—as only we *can* know—that the day will come when all
groups will become one group—one group devoted to our
Great Theory . . ." Even as he denounces the pretensions to
religious truth of all other groups, the President's speech
sounds like the proclamation of a traditional creed. Dennis
recognizes the tendency that he satirizes in his play and correctly equates the current obeisance to the psychological ma-
nipulators with the previous one to the supernatural manipu-
lators. Dennis' play is an indirect plea for the sanctity of the
individual, but it is doubtful indeed whether true individuality—self-direction and self-responsibility—has ever existed except in isolated instances. He traces what he calls the "identifying mania"—the urge to submerge one's individuality in a club
or group—to Pythagoras, whom he calls the "proto-Clubman"
and "Ur-Identifier."[9] Cassirer traces it to the Dionysian cult,
which he considers typical of "a fundamental feeling of mankind, a feeling that is common to the most primitive rites and to
the most sublime spiritualized mystic religions[:] . . . the deep

desire of the individual to be freed from the fetters of its individuality . . . to lose its identity . . ."[10] The polemic of playwrights such as Dennis is all the more intense because there is more hope for the individual than ever before. Despite the threat of the synthetic mode of life, despite the insidious onslaught of mechanization, the possibility of freedom greater than was ever thought possible before exists. Although science has been the progenitor of newer religions, it has performed the inestimable service to mankind of demonstrating the spuriousness of those based on the supernatural. Thus, although men may feel an emotional *need* for religion, they can no longer automatically attribute all ultimate knowledge and power to a postulated supernatural. Once something has been thought, as Möbius points out, it can never be unthought again. The thought, in other words, of the possibility of freedom within the individual without reference to any outside source is irreversible. Man can now ask himself whether freedom is perhaps a realization of absurdity in the Camusian sense, whether it is the compulsive and desperate carrying-on of a polemic dialectic with the environment cosmic, social, and personal. And if he has the courage to adopt that attitude he can at least escape the self-enslavement of the urge to identify and in identifying lose his identity.

Dennis conducts his polemic against the cult of the psychological guru by ridicule; and ridicule is also the method employed by José Ruibal in *El hombre y la mosca* (The Man and the Fly, 1968), the foremost play we have on the threat of the political guru. Ruibal wrote his play during the Franco dictatorship in Spain, where it was banned until after Franco's death. The play is actually about both the political and the psychological approach to the mechanization of the human being. Ruibal bases his play on a universal power figure that he calls "El Hombre." This absolute dictator has been in power for seventy years and lives in an impregnable fortress built on a foundation of the skulls of his defeated enemies. The fortress is built in the form of a dome, a symbol of the combination that has always existed historically between religion and political power. The walls of the dome are covered with trophies of hunting and of war. Like the skulls in the foundation, these are symbols of death and link the dome with the death in life that reigns in the sterile desolation outside; the inevitable result of seventy years of absolute power, absolute corruption, and hence absolute negation of life. Inside the dome the Man rules in solitude, neglecting affairs of state (the desk is piled with papers covered with a thick layer of dust), caring only about molding the populace in his own image. The Man is concerned only with his own perpetuation—that is to say, with the perpetuation of his image, for he has long since ceased to be human in the ordinary sense. To this end he is in the process of transforming a young man into his double so the people will be deluded into thinking him immortal. This involves aging the double by scarring his face and body and breaking his limbs since the Man is by this time composed mostly of prostheses.

Ruibal's skill lies in rendering the Man ludicrous and contemptible on the one hand and sinister on the other. The criticism of life that is the essential ingredient of all art is evident in the former, the recognition of reality in the latter. The Man's molding of the Double into his own image is symbolic of the political guru's need to believe that only he matters, and that those he rules must be turned into a faceless, impersonal mass. In effect, the leader becomes a machine that seeks to incorporate all those he leads. The tragedy is that those he leads cooperate willingly and fawningly in their absorption. The Double *wishes* to vanish as an individual and become an indistinguishable imitation of another person. As Dr. Johnson put it, though he did so approvingly, "Men will submit to any rule, by which they may be exempted from the tyranny of caprice and of chance. They are glad to supply by external authority their own want of constancy and resolution, and court the government of others, when long experience has convinced them of their own inability to govern themselves."[11] In Ruibal's dialectic with the reality he perceives, the Man's plan fails. When the Double takes over, he is an exact physical replica of the Man, but he does not have his spirit: appearance and manner can be changed, the inner character cannot. When he is faced with a crisis, the Double panics and destroys the dome. The dome, although made of crystal, is impenetrable from the outside but retains the fragility of glass when attacked from the inside. In addition, there is one incomplete part through which exterior elements could enter and destroy it and all it represents from the inside. In the event, a fly enters, and it is the Double's panicky attempt to kill it by shooting it that brings the dome down. Ruibal, like Dennis, writes with hope: the machine is imperfect. It can be destroyed and the integrity of individuality regained, even though it has become so powerful that it can be destroyed only from within. The Bastille-storming days of gaining freedom are over: to *re*gain it guile must be used.

In contrast to Ruibal and Dennis, Eduardo Quiles holds out little or no hope in his *El asalariado* (The Employee, 1969). His play is more a statement than a dialectic against the situation. It is, consequently, the clearest example of the synthetic drama that has been written to date. As his setting Quiles uses a business office in an extremely impoverished country. The three principal characters are deliberately caricaturized stereotype figures: a downtrodden and half-starved file clerk, an autocratic businessman, and a sexy and complaisant secretary. The half-starved employee gets a job in the businessman's office at wages that will ensure his remaining in that condition. The businessman, an exaggerated "boss" type, amuses himself by browbeating the employee and humiliating him while indulging in sensual interludes with his secretary. So far we have a conventional satire on the heartlessness of big business; but the whole perspective of the play is changed by the presence in the office of one other "character." In the background, dominating the whole action, is a robot who performs the same tasks as the employee but ceaselessly and much more rapidly. The boss constantly threatens the employee with being discharged if he does not do his work at the same rhythm as the robot. In other words, he both equates the employee with a machine and tries to turn him into one. That is nothing new, however. Although it was not formulated in those terms, bosses have been trying to turn men into robotlike machines ever since the Industrial Revolution and the invention of the assembly line.

Quiles's point is that this attitude is rapidly becoming out-moded. The autocratic boss is becoming a thing of the past. Unpleasant though he may be, he is human, and therefore unpredictable. He may at times recognize his employee's humanity, as, in fact, he does in the play. He, too, is less efficient than the machine. At the end three identically dressed men enter. Unlike the boss, they are unimpressive figures, devoid of personality and indistinguishable from each other in appearance. But it is evident that they are the real masters. They dismiss the employee and the secretary and order the now servilely cringing boss to obey the robot, whom they proceed to bow down to and worship as one would any god. The robot could, of course, just as easily be represented by a computer.

The new mechanized religion rests on a paradox: the worship as a suprahuman power of an artefact created by men themselves. This is, of course, arguably a description that fits traditional religion as well. Indeed, it is a necessary description if one is unable to accept divine revelation. The paradoxical aspect of the new "religion" consists in the fact that, according to the most recent theories in computer technology, the deified machine is or foreseeably soon will be capable of autonomous action and autonomous reproduction in a manner analogous to human evolution. That is, the autonomously reproduced machines of subsequent generations will be progressively su-perior to their creators. It is even surmised that continued human existence will become unnecessary. With the human being enslaved by the machine that can perform his functions almost inconceivably more efficiently, he will slowly—perhaps even rapidly—atrophy and finally die out. There will be no opportunity, in short, for the utopian vision of Shaw's *Back to Methuselah*, in which physical atrophy will be accompanied by a corresponding accession of mental development.

Together with Quiles's play, the Catalan writer Josep Benet i Jornet's *La nau* (The Ship, 1969) is the most perceptively prophetic and artistically critical play to deal with this most vital of dramatic and philosophical subjects to date. Benet's play takes place on a spaceship that has supposedly left the earth eons ago with a million people on board in order to seek "the furthest stars." Actually the ship *is* the earth, and its mission to seek the furthest stars symbolizes man's struggle to free himself from the mental superstitions imposed on him by ignorance and the physical restrictions imposed on him by those in authority who maintain themselves in power by purporting to know the answers to the mysteries of the human condition. The flight to the furthest stars, in other words, is a parable of man's historical struggle for existential freedom.

Benet's parable is based on the biblical fall of man. The spaceship's journey represents the history of mankind subsequent to the fall. The earth left behind by the ship was the Garden of Eden, which Benet sees as a state of mental torpor that precluded any possibility of human development. The ship (or journey of mental exploration) was constructed by the Scientists (freethinkers, intellectuals) who were subsequently killed by the Technicians. These now rule the ship and maintain the illusion of the continuation of the journey while actually keeping it static. The Technicians have concocted a Holy Book which teaches that the "reality" of life begins only with death and that the spirit that rules the universe has invested them with supreme power over the world as his representatives. That power is vested in their control of the spaceship's engine room, which was converted, after the murder of the Scientists, into a Holy of Holies that only the Technicians may enter. The levers that control the movement of the ship may be touched only by the Head Technician, to whom the spirit gives direct instructions. The parable of the abandonment of the Garden of Eden, here seen as a freely willed decision to seek knowledge rather than as an expulsion, and of the rise of religion as a repression of that search, is clear enough in this science-fiction version of Benet's.

The play opens with the funeral of a man who has ostensibly committed suicide but has actually been murdered by the Technicians because he penetrated to the engine room. Once an ordinary mortal enters the engine room he must be eliminated lest he tell his fellow men the secret of the Holy of Holies—which is that there is nothing there, of course. The play's protagonist, Dan, also penetrates to the engine room while investigating his friend's death, and he too will presumably be killed. But before this happens he moves the one lever that shows signs of being in use, the others having all rusted into immobility. The lever opens a window in the side of the ship, revealing the infinite spaces of the sky—i.e., revealing the reality that has been kept hidden from the people by the Technicians. Allegorically, the ship is the world closed and bounded by the arbitrary rules of religion and government. When Dan opens the window at the end, he opens up the possibilities realizable by the mind of man unfettered by the restrictions of tradition. The window looks out upon the cold, bare space where only existential freedom is possible, and where neither religion nor repressive government has any place—where there is no place for the manipulations of the technicians who make the human psyche their field of operation.

Synthetic drama is in its infancy, but it is the trend of the future. If art is, as I have argued throughout this work, a critical evaluation and attempted corrective of reality, determined in form and content by its social context as surely as are the human beings to whom it is addressed, then drama that concerns itself with the metamorphosis of man into machine is both timely and prophetic. The attempt to be admonitory as well as prophetic is what gives this new drama the dialectical tension that is present in all serious art. The remarkable perception displayed by the synthetic dramatists is that the mechanization of the human being, his merging into an amorphous soup like the molten liquid in the ladle of Ibsen's Button-Molder, is largely a self-willed act; and that this act is essentially a religious one. *Plus ça change, plus c'est la même chose:* the story of the modern drama, as we have seen it develop here, is the story of the rejection and re-creation of religion. In less than two hundred years the theater has come full circle on a trajectory propelled by existential fear. Once more man seeks to divorce himself from moral responsibility. Although he retains the forms and rituals intended to reassure him as to the existence of a metaphysical reference point, they no longer provide him with the enveloping comfort they did before the cataclysm of the French Revolution, which demonstrated to him the possibility of a completely atheistic state. Thus he has had to resort to the creation of a purely physical god, an unimaginably vast and complex reduplication of himself, a machine that he has created to recreate itself and swallow him up, his faculties being contemptibly feeble in comparison. Meanwhile he will be content to worship this creation of his own which he has unwittingly designed to replace him. The synthetic dramatist who recognizes and criticizes this peril is spiritually akin to the analytic dramatist, though his store of hope is less than in the days when Ibsen was eagerly redrawing the map of reality on the social tabula rasa that had been left when the French Revolution wiped away all the old superstitions. The function of art in the future, as the synthetic dramatist recognizes, can only be to resist the pernicious weakness endemic in the human spirit. Only, as Bertrand Russell has said, "on the firm foundations of unyielding despair can the soul's habitation henceforth be safely built."[12]

Notes

Index

Notes

Introduction

1 Alexandre Koyré, *The Astronomical Revolution*, trans. R. E. W. Maddison (London: Methuen, 1973), p. 72.

2 Arthur Koestler, *The Sleepwalkers* (New York: Macmillan, 1968), p. 200.

3 A. C. Crombie, *Augustine to Galileo: The History of Science, A.D. 400–1650* (London: Falcon Educational Books, 1952), p. 309.

4 Koestler, *Sleepwalkers*, p. 195.

5 Ibid., p. 215.

6 Francis Cornford, *The Unwritten Philosophy* (Cambridge: Cambridge University Press, 1950), p. 45. It is not too much to say, indeed, that the discoveries of Copernicus, Kepler, and Galileo were "the most important turning point in man's history; and . . . caused a more radical change in his mode of existence than the acquisition of a third eye or some other biological mutation could have achieved" (Koestler, *Sleepwalkers*, pp. 112–13).

7 Paul H. Michel, *The Cosmology of Giordano Bruno*, trans. R. E. W. Maddison (Ithaca, N.Y.: Cornell University Press, 1973), p. 29.
8 Crombie, *Augustine to Galileo*, p. 324.
9 Koestler, *Sleepwalkers*, pp. 191–92.
10 Ibid., p. 215.
11 Quoted in William Boulting, *Giordano Bruno* (New York: E. P. Dutton, [1916]), p. 141.
12 Quoted in William Barrett, *Irrational Man* (Garden City, N.Y.: Doubleday, 1958), p. 99.
13 Quoted in ibid., p. 104. Kepler had remarked, "The infinite is unthinkable" when told of Galileo's astronomical discoveries (Koestler, *Sleepwalkers*, p. 367).
14 Blaise Pascal, *Pensées*, trans. H. F. Stewart (New York: Panthéon Books, 1950), p. 30. ("Condition de l'homme: inconstance, ennuy, inquiétude.")
15 Ibid., pp. 172–73. ("Le silence éternel de ces espaces infinis m'effraye.")
16 Erich Heller, *The Disinherited Mind* (New York: Farrar, Straus and Cudahy, 1957), p. 218.
17 The relevant passage is sec. 108 of *Die fröhliche Wissenschaft:* "God is dead; but given the way of men, there may still be caves for thousands of years in which his shadow will be shown. —And we—we still have to vanquish his shadow, too" (Friedrich Nietzsche, *The Gay Science*, trans. Walter Kaufmann, [New York: Vintage Books, 1974], p. 167).
18 Ibid., p. 182 (sec. 125).
19 Cf. ibid., p. 182 and 279 (secs. 126 and 343).
20 Synthesis, the third philosophical attitude to be found in modern drama, is a very recent development. Its name indicates both that it is a synthesis of the first two attitudes and that it deals with a synthetic, i.e., mechanical, solution to philosophical problems. It will be dealt with in the third part of the book.
21 Barrett, *Irrational Man*, p. 20.
22 Ibid., p. 21.
23 These attitudes correspond, roughly, to Dadaism, expressionism, and surrealism, respectively.

CHAPTER 1: Fragmentation

1 Victor Svanberg, "The Strindberg Cult," in Otto Reinert, ed.,

Strindberg: A Collection of Critical Essays (Englewood Cliffs, N.J.: Prentice-Hall, 1971), pp. 71–72.

2 August Strindberg, *Eight Expressionist Plays*, trans. Arvid Paulson (New York: New York University Press, 1965), p. 163.

3 Ibid., p. 165

4 August Strindberg, *Inferno, Alone and Other Writings*, trans. and ed. Evert Sprinchorn (Garden City, N.Y.: Anchor Books, 1968), pp. 235–36.

5 Cf. Carl Dahlström, *Strindberg's Dramatic Expressionism* (Ann Arbor: University of Michigan Press, 1930).

6 Paulson, in Strindberg, *Eight Expressionist Plays*, pp. 262–63.

7 Ibid., p. 292.

8 Evert Sprinchorn, "The Logic of *A Dream Play*," in Reinert, *Strindberg*, p. 138.

9 Ibid., p. 150.

10 Strindberg, *Eight Expressionist Plays*, p. 343.

11 Quoted in Oscar Büdel, *Pirandello* (New York: Hillary House, 1966), p. 14.

12 Ibid., p. 9.

13 Cf. Albert Bermel, *Contradictory Characters* (New York: E. P. Dutton, 1975), pp. 122–43.

14 Ibid., pp. 2, 288.

15 The argument against Pirandello's concept of theater is effectively summed up in Ortega y Gasset's statement that ". . . an object of art is artistic only in so far as it is not real." Ortega goes on to give as an example Titian's portrait of Charles V on horseback. He claims, correctly, I believe, that in order to enjoy it "we must forget that this is Charles the Fifth in person and see instead a portrait—that is, an image, a fiction. The portrayed person and his portrait are two entirely different things; we are interested in either one or the other. In the first case we 'live' with Charles the Fifth, in the second we look at an object of art" (José Ortega y Gasset, *The Dehumanization of Art* [Garden City, N.Y.: Doubleday, 1956], p. 10). The same principle holds as true of the actor as of the painting of Charles V: the person who looks on the painting as Charles V qua Charles V would look on the portrayal of Hamlet as either a real, living person named Hamlet, current heir to the throne of Denmark (a view encouraged by the mania for modern-dress productions) or as Laurence Olivier—or whoever may be playing the part—inexplicably prancing, cavorting, and spouting archaic verse.

16 E. F. Benson, *As We Were* (Harmondsworth: Penguin Books, 1938), p. 223.

17 Translated by the present writer in Michael Benedikt and George E. Wellwarth, eds., *Modern French Theatre* (New York: E. P. Dutton, 1964), p. 225.

18 For a full critical discussion of Jarry, see my *Theatre of Protest and Paradox* (New York: New York University Press, 1971), pp. 1–14.

19 From an account of a conversation with Freud in Stefan Zweig, *The World of Yesterday* (Lincoln: University of Nebraska Press, 1971), p. 424.

20 William Butler Yeats, *Autobiography* (Garden City, N.Y.: Doubleday, 1958), pp. 233–34.

21 I refer here to the graphic depiction of cruelty—frequently unsimulated—in such plays as Kenneth Brown's *The Brig* and other Living Theatre productions.

22 Roger Shattuck, *The Banquet Years* (Garden City, N.Y.: Anchor Books, 1961), p. 243.

23 Quoted in ibid., p. 242.

24 Alfred Jarry, *La chandelle verte,* ed. Maurice Saillet (Paris: Livre de Poche, 1969), pp. 421–25.

25 Alfred Jarry, "Exploits and Opinions of Dr. Faustroll, Pataphysician," *Evergreen Review* 4, no. 13 (1960), 134–37.

26 Eugene Ionesco, *Notes et contre-notes* (Paris: Gallimard, 1962), p. 7.

27 Malcolm Cowley, "The Religion of Art," *New Republic,* January 10, 1934, p. 247.

28 Manuel Grossman, *Dada* (New York: Pegasus Press, 1971), p. 87.

29 Translated by the present writer in Michael Benedikt and George E. Wellwarth, eds., *Post War German Theatre* (New York: E. P. Dutton, 1967), p. 255.

30 Translated by Michael Benedikt in Benedikt & Wellwarth, *Modern French Theatre,* p. 133.

31 André Breton, *Qu'est-ce que le surréalisme?* quoted in Maurice Nadeau, *Histoire du surréalisme* (Paris: Seuil, 1945), p. 19.

32 Ibid., pp. 29–31.

33 Ibid., p. 17.

34 Quoted in Maurice Nadeau, *Documents surréalistes* (Paris: Seuil, 1948), p. 15.

35 Mary Anne Caws, *André Breton* (New York: Twayne, 1971), p. 13.

36 Ibid., p. 25.

37 Quoted in ibid., pp. 24–25.

38 Nadeau, *Documents surréalistes*, p. 42.
39 Ibid., p. 45.
40 René Daumal, *Mount Analogue*, trans. Roger Shattuck (New York: Pantheon Books, 1959), p. 52.
41 Ibid.
42 Ibid. Italics in original.
43 Ibid., pp. 42–49. Italics mine.
44 Ibid., p. 132.
45 I assume he would not have maintained his jejune Marxism for long.
46 Christopher Caudwell, *The Concept of Freedom* (London: Lawrence & Wishart, 1965), p. 197.
47 Ibid., p. 195.
48 Albert Camus, *Le mythe de Sisyphe* (Paris: Gallimard, 1942), p. 15.
49 Ibid., p. 17.
50 Friedrich Dürrenmatt, *Die Wiedertäufer* (Zürich: Verlag der Arche, 1967), p. 101.

CHAPTER 2: Analysis

1 Henry James, *The Scenic Art* (New Brunswick, N.J.: Rutgers University Press, 1948), p. 243.
2 Bernard Shaw, *Complete Plays with Prefaces* (New York: Dodd, Mead, 1962), 5:192.
3 Henrik Ibsen, *Brand,* trans. Michael Meyer (London: Rupert Hart-Davis, 1960), pp. 53, 58, 59.
4 F. L. Lucas, *The Drama of Ibsen and Strindberg* (New York: Macmillan, 1962), p. 97.
5 Georg Groddeck, *"Peer Gynt"* in Rolf Fjelde, ed., *Ibsen* (Englewood Cliffs, N.J.: Prentice-Hall, 1965), p. 78. Italics mine.
6 Ibid., p. 79.
7 Brian Downs, *A Study of Six Plays by Ibsen* (Cambridge: Cambridge University Press, 1950), p. 82; and James Hurt, *Catiline's Dream* (Urbana: University of Illinois Press, 1972), p. 65.
8 Francis Bull, *Ibsen: The Man and the Dramatist* (Oxford: Clarendon Press, 1954), p. 5.
9 Ibid., p. 7.
10 Ibid., p. 5. Italics mine.

11 Quotations are from act 2, scene 7, Henrik Ibsen, *Eleven Plays* (New York: Modern Library, n.d.), p. 1083.
12 Downs, *Study of Six Plays by Ibsen*, p. 96. Downs mentions Goethe's attitude to Faust, Byron's to Don Juan, and Schiller's to William Tell as examples.
13 Henrik Ibsen, *Ghosts and Three Other Plays*, trans. Michael Meyer (Garden City, N.Y.: Anchor Books, 1966), p. [vii].
14 Downs, *Study of Six Plays by Ibsen*, p. 118.
15 Henrik Ibsen, *Eleven Plays*, pp. 185–86.
16 Downs, *Study of Six Plays by Ibsen*, p. 152.
17 Henrik Ibsen, *Hedda Gabler and Three Other Plays*, trans. Michael Meyer (Garden City, N.Y.: Anchor Books, 1961), p. 183.
18 Ibsen, *Hedda Gabler and Three Other Plays*, p. 266.
19 Ibsen, *Ghosts and Three Other Plays*, pp. 341–42.
20 Ibid., p. 342.
21 Bernard Shaw, *Complete Plays with Prefaces* (New York: Dodd, Mead, 1962), 3:486.
22 Ibid., p. ix.
23 Ibid., 1:68.
24 William Irvine, ed., *Bernard Shaw: Selected Plays and Other Writings* (New York: Rinehart, 1956), p. xx.
25 Shaw, *Complete Plays with Prefaces*, 5:479. Italics mine.
26 Katherine Haynes Gatch, "The Last Plays of Shaw: Dialectic and Despair," in Warren Smith, ed., *Bernard Shaw's Plays* (New York: W. W. Norton, 1970), p. 470.
27 Shaw, *Complete Plays with Prefaces*, 5:493–94.
28 Ibid., 6:533.
29 Ibid.
30 Ibid., 5:493 (Preface to *On the Rocks*). It is significant that this attitude is not a development of Shaw's disillusioned old age. As early as 1906 in the preface to *Major Barbara* he was proposing the same things—and in almost the same words: "It would be far more sensible to put up with their vices, as we put up with their illnesses, until they give more trouble than they are worth, at which point we should, with many apologies and expressions of sympathy, and some generosity in complying with their last wishes, place them in the lethal chamber and get rid of them" (ibid., 1:337). Note that the courtesy of being apologetic to the condemned man dates from 1906.
31 Ibid., 6:531–32 (Preface to *The Simpleton*).

32 Ibid., 5:524.
33 Dan H. Laurence, ed., *Platform and Pulpit* (New York: Hill & Wang, 1961), p. 258.
34 Bertolt Brecht, *Baal, A Man's A Man, and The Elephant Calf*, ed. Eric Bentley (New York: Grove Press, 1964), pp. 14 and 10.
35 Ibid., p. 59. Bentley's translation.
36 Bertolt Brecht, *The Jewish Wife and Other Short Plays* (New York: Grove Press, 1965), p. 108. Bentley's translation.
37 Ibid., p. 79.
38 Eric Bentley, *Theatre of War* (New York: Viking Press, 1973), p. 167.
39 Bertolt Brecht, *Seven Plays*, ed. Eric Bentley (New York: Grove Press, 1961), p. 586.
40 Ibid., pp. 586–87.
41 Bertolt Brecht, *Stücke* (Berlin: Suhrkamp Verlag, 1962), 8:201.
42 Ibid., p. 205.
43 Ibid., pp. 206–7.
44 Brecht, *Seven Plays*, pp. 399–400.
45 Ibid., p. 354.
46 Jean-Paul Sartre, *The Flies*, trans. Stuart Gilbert in Jean-Paul Sartre, *No Exit and Three Other Plays* (New York: Vintage Books, n.d.), p. 103.

CHAPTER 3: Synthesis

1 Friedrich Dürrenmatt, *Die Physiker* (Zürich: Verlag der Arche, 1962), pp. 61–62. My translation.
2 Ibid., p. 63.
3 Ibid., p. 68.
4 Georg Büchner, *Woyzeck*, trans. George E. Wellwarth, in George E. Wellwarth, ed., *Themes of Drama* (New York: Thomas Y. Crowell, 1973), p. 566.
5 Barrett R. Clark, ed., *European Theories of the Drama* (New York: Crown, 1966), p. 536.
6 Xavier Fàbregas, "Proleg," in Manuel de Pedrolo, *Darrera versió, per ara* (Barcelona: Edicions 62, 1971), p. 5. My translation.
7 Ibid., p. 17.
8 Ernst Cassirer, *The Myth of the State* (New Haven: Yale University Press, 1946), p. 286.

9 Nigel Dennis, *Two Plays and a Preface* (New York: Vantage Press, 1958), p. 30.
10 Cassirer, *Myth of the State*, p. 41.
11 James Boswell, *Life of Johnson* (London: Oxford University Press, 1960), p. 258.
12 Bertrand Russell, *Mysticism and Logic* (New York: W. W. Norton, c. 1929), p. 46.

Index

174   Index

COMPOSED BY MODERN TYPOGRAPHERS OF FLORIDA, INC.
DUNEDIN, FLORIDA
MANUFACTURED BY CUSHING MALLOY, INC.
ANN ARBOR, MICHIGAN
TEXT AND DISPLAY LINES ARE SET IN BASKERVILLE

Library of Congress Cataloging-in-Publication Data
Wellwarth, George E., 1932–
Modern drama and the death of God.
Includes bibliographical references and index.
1. Drama—20th century—History and criticism.
2. God in literature.   3. Religion and literature.
I. Title.
PN1861.W38   1986   809.2'04   86-40064
ISBN 0-299-10850-3